Women Writers
of the West Coast

Speaking of Their Lives and Careers

Women Writers
of the West Coast

Speaking of Their Lives and Careers

EDITED AND INTRODUCED BY
Marilyn Yalom

PHOTOGRAPHS BY
Margo Davis

*Prepared under the auspices of the
Center for Research on Women,
Stanford University*

Capra Press
SANTA BARBARA

Text Copyright ©1983 Marilyn Yalom.
Photographs ©1983 by Margo Davis.
Printed in the United States of America.
All rights reserved.
Published by Capra Press
P.O. Box 2068
Santa Barbara, California 93120

Cover Design by Francine Rudesill
Design and Typography by Jim Cook/Santa Barbara

Library of Congress Cataloging in Publication Data
WOMEN WRITERS OF THE WEST COAST.
"Prepared under the auspices of the Center for Research on Women, Stanford University."
Includes bibliographies.
Contents: Maxine Hong Kingston—Janet Lewis—
Joyce Carol Thomas—[etc.]
1. Women authors, American—Pacific coast (North
America)—Interviews. 2. Women authors, American—20th
century—Interviews. 3. Authorship. 4. Pacific coast
(North America) in literature. 5. West (U.S.) in
literature. I. Yalom, Marilyn. II. Davis, Margo
Baumgarten. III. Title.
PS281.W65 1983   810'.9'9287   83-15005
ISBN 0-88496-204-0

CONTENTS

PREFACE

This book grew out of a series of public dialogues with Janet Lewis, Joyce Carol Thomas, Tillie Olsen, Ursula LeGuin, Susan Griffin, Jessamyn West and Judy Grahn at Stanford University in the fall of 1980. Three off-stage conversations with Maxine Hong Kingston, Kay Boyle and Diane Johnson supplemented the public series. Sponsored by Stanford's Center for Research on Women, the project brought together prominent West Coast women writers and Stanford-based interviewers. Subsequently, transcripts of all the interviews were edited so as to focus more exclusively on the writers.

I wish to take this occasion to thank the many people and organizations who contributed to the realization of this book: the writers and interviewers who gave generously of their time to plan and enact the dialogues and who helped edit their respective chapters; the staff of the Center for Research on Women who bore with me throughout the various versions of the manuscript; Margo Davis who helped conceive the initial project and produced the superb photographic portraits of each writer; Jennifer Chapman who helped coordinate the public series with steadfast efficiency and good cheer; the California Council for the Humanities and the California Arts Council which provided financial support; and Noel Young who believed in the value of turning awkward transcripts into readable prose and showed me how to do it.

—MARILYN YALOM
Center for Research on Women
Stanford University
May 1983

INTRODUCTION

"Writing takes so much determination—you would do it on a rock in the middle of the ocean, if you had to." Speaking of her own commitment to writing, poet Judy Grahn expressed the stubborn will that animates all the writers in this book. Their life stories speak of persistence in the face of awesome obstacles: poverty, illness, close encounters with death, and the social, psychological and economic fetters specific to women, such as those inherent in the raising of children.

Yet each author also speaks of special circumstances that encouraged the creative process: the sustenance provided by mothers, fathers, friends, husbands and lovers; the support of the feminist community; the beneficent influence of life on the West Coast where, according to Susan Griffin, one's outlook is not so bound in tradition as it would be in the East.

The influence of the Western setting is far-reaching. Janet Lewis is inspired to write of the Sierras and John Muir, "patron saint of the mountains." Jessamyn West, finding she "could not tolerate a land where earth and sky did not meet," returns happily to the openness of the West. Ursula LeGuin places her imaginative utopias in barren landscapes like the moon, in direct contrast to the sunny reality of her native California. Susan Griffin, raised in California like West and LeGuin, becomes a mystic through her life-long contact with an accessible nature. Conversely, Diane Johnson, whose urban "nests" stretch from San Francisco and Berkeley to London, chooses Los Angeles as the setting for one of her most frightening novels because it is a "scary" city where anything untoward can easily be imagined.

Some speak of the special social and political forces found in the West. Kay Boyle recalls her involvement in the anti-war movement at San Francisco State University where she taught in the sixties. Tillie Olsen, Susan Griffin and Judy Grahn are identified with the feminist movement of the seventies that found so nurturing a home in the Bay area. Maxine Hong Kingston writes of the Chinese American communities of her youth in Stockton, Berkeley and San Francisco, and the tales told of a mythical China. Joyce Carol Thomas, whose roots are in the Black South and who has yet to write of her California years, speaks of the supportive context provided by other Bay area women, such as the poet Josephine Miles.

All express their admiration for other women writers: Virginia

Woolf, Colette, Marianne Moore, Carson McCullers, Emily
Dickinson, George Sand, Gertrude Stein, Toni Morrison, Grace
Paley, Maya Angelou, Toni Cade Bambara, Doris Lessing, Jean Wolf,
Vonda McIntyre, Jessica Mitford, Alison Lurie, Adrienne Rich, the
Brontës, Joan Didion, Alice Adams, Sheila Ballantyre, without
discounting the influence of certain male writers as well. Sometimes
they cite each other. It is curiously satisfying for me to see, in the
penultimate chapter of this book, Kay Boyle at the age of eighty
tipping her hat to Maxine Hong Kingston, who is half her age and
who appears in the book's first chapter. Their concern with the
writings of their female predecessors and contemporaries seems to
substantiate the theory, first espoused by the critic Ellen Moers,*
that women writers look to each other for the creation and
maintenance of a common literary tradition.

Certain issues crop up in almost all the chapters. What does it
mean to be a "woman" writer? To what extent does each of these
writers consider herself a "feminist"? How does the writer translate a
particular experience into a vision that has meaning for other
human beings? What are the boundaries between the lived experience and the world of the imagination? Although the questions are
often the same, the answers are varied, reflecting generational, class
and tempermental differences in the ten lives. Thus Boyle, Lewis
and West, all in their eighties, tend to minimize the importance of
the feminist movement, which Grahn, Griffin and Kingston, at the
age of forty, recognize as crucial in the formation of their adult
sensibilities.

Similarly, two camps emerged along socio-economic lines.
Most of the older writers, with the exception of Olsen, bear the
mark of the relatively affluent, educated milieux in which they
were raised, whereas most of the younger writers identified themselves as "working class," "common" or "minority women." As
examples of this difference in formation and orientation, it is
instructive to compare two poems by Janet Lewis and Judy Grahn
quoted in the book.

Lewis, in her poem "Awatobi," finds a commonality in the
bloody violence of an American Indian battle and a political reprisal
in seventeenth century France. The poem contains reference to
Purcell, Racine, the Huguenots, and Madame de Maintenon—
references wasted on anyone unfamiliar with the details of French

*(Ellen Moers, *Literary Women* [Garden City, New York: Anchor Books, 1977].)

history. Lewis's carefully cadenced style is subtle and ironic; she evokes the rarified culture of the court of Louis XIV as counterpoint to the human savagery that erupts among the "civilized" French as well as the "uncivilized" Indians.

In contrast, Judy Grahn, in her poem "Vera, from my childhood," confronts the reader head-on with a defiant vision of the common woman rising "as the best of bread." Grahn's poetics derive both from her personal experience as a woman of the people and from the co-opting of a populist, Whitmanesque tradition into the service of the female sex. Her poems are woman-oriented and lesbian, yet intended "for everyone."

Like Grahn, several of the writers see themselves as inheritors and creators of an oral tradition. Tillie Olsen says of herself: "I am primarily an oral/aural writer...I use the 'mother tongue' primarily, the language of the deepest, purest emotion, language that does not come primarily out of books..." Griffin based her play *Voices* on the spoken language of characters who "so much wanted to tell their stories," and she constructed her book *Women and Nature* in the form of a spoken dialogue between an authoritarian, masculine voice and a female voice struggling to be heard. Thomas remembers the storytelling that took place during her childhood at the time of the cotton harvest and the sermons of fundamentalist Black preachers as key influences on her fiction and poetry. Kingston speaks of the difficulties of reconstructing the language of illiterate peasants in a small Chinese village: "it's a matter of starting with a language that has no writing and yet writing about people who talk-story in that language." This group of writers is particularly concerned with the struggle to bring into literature previously stilled, predominantly female, and largely unschooled voices.

If, as Kay Boyle believes, no one writer has yet emerged in the West to rival such Paris-thirties luminaries as Joyce and Stein, still it is impossible to ignore the flowering of literature on the West Coast and to discount the significant contribution made by women writers. Despite the diversity of their styles and life experiences, all the authors attest to the extraordinary vigor of the female voice in our time and place.

Maxine Hong Kingston

FROM AN INTERVIEW BETWEEN KINGSTON
AND ARTURO ISLAS, PROFESSOR OF ENGLISH, STANFORD UNIVERSITY,
OCTOBER 1, 1980, BERKELEY, CALIFORNIA.

Since the publication of *The Woman Warrior* and *China Men*, Maxine Hong Kingston has been declared one of Hawaii's national treasures. She has lived in Hawaii for the past decade with her husband Earl and their son, after a girlhood in Stockton, California, and young adult years in Berkeley. For her readers, however, her spiritual homeland which she describes eloquently in the portraits of her Chinese ancestors—real and imagined—is located in what she calls "the small tradition of China."

Conversing with her in the kitchen of a friend's home in Berkeley, we are transported to the peasant tradition from which springs her particular form of story-telling, of "talk-story." Maxine Hong Kingston's small stature belies her lioness-like intensity. She makes coffee while she thinks and then answers a question about being an "ethnic" writer. She speaks carefully, her voice quiet and clear. Her hands are very expressive.

"There is an expectation among readers and critics that I *should* represent the race. I don't like hearing non-Chinese people say to a Chinese person, 'Well now I know about you because I have read Maxine Hong Kingston's books.' Each artist has a unique voice. Many readers don't understand that. The problem of how representative one is will only be solved when we have many more Chinese American writers. Then readers will see how diverse our people are. Black writers have already surmounted the problem.

"Of course, there are Chinese American writers who seek to represent the rest of us; they end up with tourist manuals or chamber of commerce public relations whitewash. What I look forward to is the time when many of us are published and then we will be able to see the range of viewpoints, of visions, of what it is to be Chinese American." She pauses and then adds, "I have asked my sisters, 'On a range of one to ten how odd do you think we were? How odd was our upbringing?' One of them said we were an eight and that means pretty odd, which is to say that we are not very representative of Chinese Americans."

She explains how in her books she writes about one small village in South China which is not representative of greater China. From that village, a few people came to America and settled in Stockton. "A Stockton Chinese is not the same as a San Francisco Chinese. I know that if I write about some very particular custom, some people will say, 'No, we don't have that custom at all.'" She calls the entire issue of being a representative ethnic writer "very bothersome." Her own resolution to the problem has been to give expression to her own vision. "Because that's what's interesting— the way one person sees the world. It's up to other people to ask themselves whether they think like that or not. And if they don't think like you, that should be very exciting to them. They would read about something that they are completely unfamiliar with. I just visited Hong Kong and loved seeing Chinese who were different from myself. To think of the possibility of another way of being Chinese or of being a human being is much more exciting than to see someone just like me."

She asks Islas what he has learned about "ethnic" writing from reading her work. As someone who has been identified as an ethnic writer himself, Islas, a Mexican American, says that it is instructive to see how she taps her sources, which are Chinese, in such a way as to make that world accessible to those who are not at all familiar with it. Though she rejects the notion of being a "representative" writer, no one can walk the streets of Chinatown or any Chinese neighborhood after reading her work without new insights.

Speaking of the problems inherent in being an "ethnic" writer, Kingston says, "One of the problems in writing the books was to figure out what to do with the language. So many of the people are not speaking English or they speak it with an accent. They use Chinese words, and they aren't just speaking Chinese-Chinese. They're speaking Chinese with an American change in the language, and also they are speaking the dialect of one little village. So what are you going to do to give the readers a sense of this language without just repeating it because then nobody will understand it? That's an example of the artistic problems you encounter when you deal with a culture that has not been adequately portrayed before. I'm also writing about poor people in another subculture. Are poor people representative?"

Then, referring to the tradition from which she springs: "All the mythology in *China Men* is from what the Chinese call the small tradition, not the great literary traditions, but those of lower class people. When I write, I think of them in the language of the peasants of one particular village, and that language has not been written down. I write about illiterate people whose language has not even been Romanized. So it's a matter of starting with a language that has no writing and yet writing about people who talk-story in that language."

When asked if there were any central event in her life that served as the origins of her books, Kingston answers: "I don't think there was a single precipitating event. My writing is an ongoing function, like breathing or eating. I started writing as a child. I'd write down anything and these two books are just part of the things I wrote. I have this habit of writing things down. Anything. And then some of it falls into place, as in these two books." She does not show her work to other people while she is writing. "Just as I basically keep things to myself in general," she adds.

She was fortunate to have had both of her books, and especially the first, immediately accepted for publication. She had been writing *The Woman Warrior* for two and a half years before she showed it to an agent. "But that is a deceptively short time. I was writing these books as a child, but I didn't have the ability or maturity. A kid doesn't yet have the vocabulary, though I had the feelings. In some sense, you could say that I was working on these books for twenty or thirty years, but in another sense, I wrote them just a few years ago."

Was she surprised by their instant reception and acclaim? "Sometimes I am surprised. Other times I think, 'Well, of course,' because what keeps you going as a writer are the fantasies of that big-selling book. But I was surprised when both books were on the best-seller list at the same time. It never occurred to me that *that* could happen."

What have been her relatives' reactions to her work? "Because my family is so large, there has been a wide range of reactions. My parents neither speak nor read English, so they don't have an accurate sense of what I have written. My brothers and sisters are the people I feel closest to; they are most like me. And their reactions are very satisfying because they can talk about my work in a way that makes sense to me. They'll remember an event that I write about and they'll think what I wrote is very funny. That is satisfying to me because a lot of people don't understand the humor in my work. I guess when people come to ethnic writing, they have such a reverence for it or are so scared that they don't want to laugh. But my brothers and sisters say 'Oh, this is really funny' or remember an event in the same way. Though sometimes there's disagreement, like when one brother said 'That wasn't opium the men were smoking,' and my other brother said 'Oh yes, it was. That *was* opium.' And I like that difference in seeing because it could have been either way; one remembered it one way and one the other. That gives me two stories for one event.

"There are also some relatives who feel I have revealed 'family secrets.' For example, there is an aunt who said, 'How could you be so nasty!' But I felt she was unfair, that kind of reaction usually comes from people who don't finish the book. They read the beginning and don't understand that things are resolved by the end. There *is* a lot of resolution—the mother and daughter come out okay, you know. But it's at the price of a lifetime of struggle. I think that a few of my cousins don't understand that; they get to the hard part and stop reading."

She was also disturbed by the critic in the *New York Review of Books* who said that she was attempting to connect her family and Chinese Americans in general to the great high tradition of China by writing its myths. "These people tell peasant myths to one another, they pass them on and derive their strength from them. They also derive their doubts by comparing themselves to heroes of the past. I know all of these great heroes from the high tradition and they're not helping me in my American life. Such myths need to be changed and integrated into the peasant's life as well as into the Chinese American's life. And, don't forget, the myths change from one telling to another." In her eyes, the New York critic failed to grasp this essential quality in her work and method of story-telling.

Sinologists also do not seem to understand what she is doing in her portrayal of Chinese American characters and, in particular, the language they speak. "There are some grandfathers in *China Men* who obviously must have a name just like everybody else, like the names their parents gave them, but I call them 'great-grandfather' and 'great-great-grandfather,' because that's what I actually call them, that's how they were known in the family. Also, it was the custom for children *not* to know the names of their parents and grandparents. I decided to use the name 'grandfather' because I thought that all of us see them as ancestors, the grandfathers and great-grandfathers who are like mythical characters of the past golden age. These people would have died before we were born or in our childhood. We saw them as big and we were little. We know their stories as great stories; they are almost like people we read about in books or in mythology. They are far from us, and so I decided that it was all right just to call them 'great-grandfather' because they become the great-grandfather of us all. Also, they become the great-grandfathers of our country in the sense of claiming America. I didn't go into it in much detail in *China Men* but many Chinese have a baby name given to them by their parents; when they grow up they choose an adult name, one associated with an ability or feat. People often change a name to celebrate a change in their lives. Then most who come to the United States have an American name. Chinese are also good at nicknames. Naming tells the world who you are. It also gives a new American identity; and one musn't forget the paper names for the immigration service. People don't seem to understand what I am doing. For example, a sinologist might review my book and not even mention that I don't spell the words right. I don't spell them the way you would find them in a Cantonese dictionary or in a Mandarin dictionary because I decided to spell them in a new way, because Americans would speak in this new way. A Chinese scholar should say, 'Hey, she's got it all wrong' but they don't seem to understand.

"There are quite a few other Chinese American writers. They just haven't gotten the publicity I have, but it's important to remember that I am not an exception. I'm not the only one who can use the language. There are new writers publishing all the time, for example, a new mystery writer named Tony Chew, who wrote a book called *Port Arthur Chicken*. Laurence Yep has published at least six books—children's books and science fiction. And the playwright David Hwang has written a play called *FOB* which is wonderful! Working independently, we came to many of the same images. He shows two characters having a food race; they put hot sauces on their food and compete to see who can eat this hot sauce the fastest. I had a food race in *China Men* too and I thought, while watching David's play, 'That's right. We are right.' Chinese are so interested in food, and he saw it and I saw it, and it means that we both are authentic. Just a little detail like that...."

When asked if, as a Chinese American woman writer, she was somehow seen as a traitor to the village or clan in the same light as the "No-Name Woman" who is portrayed so poignantly in the first chapter of *The Woman Warrior*, she replied: "For people who know me, it is a very normal thing that I would write these books. Those who don't know me have criticized me—critics, strangers, scholars, some Chinese American males who use my work for their own political purposes. In a way, I don't connect with that kind of criticism because I don't think they are talking about me or my work. Some people have said that the white male press or publishing industry will publish women, but they'll castrate male writers. They go on to say that this is why we don't have a major novelist among Asian Americans. That has been a charge against me, as if somehow I were in collusion with the white publishers in America."

When she writes, she does not have a Chinese American audience in mind. "I am really a megalomaniac because I write for everybody living today and people in the future; that's my audience, for generations." She learned this kind of impartiality from fifteen years of teaching in California and Hawaii where students who can't read are placed in the same classroom with geniuses. "Each one is your student—you must teach so that it means something to every student, so that you are valuable as a teacher to each one of them."

Kingston describes herself as a West Coast Chinese American. "I am very West Coast. I really feel West Coast, like Central Valley, as distinguished from San Francisco. I don't identify with San Francisco. Stockton, Sacramento, Fresno, all of the Valley in the north—Steinbeck's land. That reminds me, I read *Cannery Row* very carefully. I wanted to see how he did certain things. At the end of *Cannery Row*, there is a party where somebody recites a poem, and it doesn't stop the dramatic action. I studied how he did that because I wanted to quote some songs and poems without stopping the drama."

William Carlos Williams was also cited as a significant influence. His work *The American Dream* was inspirational for her conception of what it means to claim America in a literary way. Does "claiming America" mean assimilation of American values? "No. I mean it as a response to the legislation and racism that says we of Chinese origin do not belong here in America. It's a response to the assumption that I come from Vietnam or another Asian country. When I say I am a native American with all the rights of an American, I am saying, 'No, we're not outsiders; we Chinese belong here. This is our country, this is our history, we are a part of America. If it weren't for us, America would be a different place.'"

Does he think of herself as a feminist? "I have always been a feminist but feminism is just one modern political stance, like being an ethnic writer. One has to have an even larger vision. I don't think my writing would limit itself to whatever is politically useful."

Nonetheless, Kingston agreed that *The Woman Warrior* gave expression to significant feminist concerns, such as the brutally inequitable treatment of women in traditional Chinese society and the complex relationship of daughter to mother. At the end of *The Woman Warrior*, the resolution that takes place between the mother and daughter is linked to the feminist issue of breaking female silence. The daughter becomes the inheritor of the mother's oral tradition, which subsequently becomes a written tradition. Kingston revealed that the problem of finding a speaking and writing voice had great personal meaning. "I went through a time when I did not talk to people. It's still happening to me but not so severely. I'm all right now but I do know people who never came out of it."

She conceded that the little speechless girl in the book was in some way a double for herself. "But she is also based on somebody I know, who is a recluse today in that Victorian-woman sense. Even today, she is that closed off. Now I'm talking about people who grew up in the forties and fifties. When I wrote that story, I thought: I am writing about my generation of Chinese Americans. But I am very startled when I now speak at colleges, and people in the audience—educators, psychologists, teachers—tell me that they are working with people like that *right now*. This is an ongoing problem with people who are trying to figure out what to do when the home culture is different from the public culture. I guess what happens to some people is that they are just shocked into silence.

"Language is important to our sanity. *You have to be able to tell your story, you have to be able to make up stories or you go mad.* This is what happens with Moon Orchid who comes from Mainland China after the war and doesn't speak English. Part of sanity is to be able to understand the language of other people, and also I think that even when people aren't mad, sometimes when you hear two people speaking in another language, you get a little bit of paranoia. 'Are they saying something about me?' And we sane people feel like that! So, when Moon Orchid goes over the edge, that same tendency is exaggerated, and I am hinting that perhaps if she spoke the language, it might have saved her."

Maxine Hong Kingston views writing as a continuous process, so that even the periods of inactivity are fruitful. At the time of the interview, she had no work in progress because she had decided to take time off after *The Woman Warrior* and *China Men*. "Just to see what happens in the subconscious because I worked for seven years on those two books. You go into the subconscious by not writing and then you make it normal consciousness by writing. Then you rewrite until you are working almost mechanically—the grammar and the structure are all mental and rational. Now is my time for not doing any writing. I mean to get far into the subconscious where there are no word sequences."

This view of writing also derives from her great respect for the oral tradition which she sees as very much alive. "It has the impact of command, of directly influencing action. Also, the oral stories change from telling to telling. It changes according to the needs of the listener, according to the needs of the day, the interest of the time, so that the story can be different from day to day. What happens when you write it down? Writing is static. The story will remain as printed for the next two hundred years and it's not going to change. That really bothers me, because what would be wonderful would be for the words to change on the page every time, but they can't. The way I tried to solve this problem was to keep ambiguity in the writing all the time.

"Students want you to come to class and tell them, 'Yes, I was that silent girl,' or they want me to say, 'Yes, I have this aunt, Moon Orchid.' They want that. But what I want is to see the stories change. Maybe Moon Orchid is like this today, but tomorrow I'm going to tell you something else that she did. I try to keep that extra little doubt in the stories. I throw it in. I can't help it, it seems to be part of every story."

Among others, Henry James would have felt a shock of recognition hearing her insist on the ambiguity within her work. She tells a marvelous anecdote to illustrate her point: "Did you know that in some Asian cities—I know this happened in Singapore, but probably less so now—there are storytellers who walk into a restaurant and come to your table and tell you a story. Then, just before the climax, they will stop telling the story until you pay them. And after you pay them, they tell you the ending. The more money you pay, the better the ending!"

Then, with characteristic modesty, she says, "I feel so bad sometimes thinking of this great oral tradition, and along comes Most of their tradition was oral and then someone came along and wrote it down."

MAXINE HONG KINGSTON, 1940–

Selected Bibliography

Fiction (memoirs)

WOMAN WARRIOR: MEMOIRS OF A GIRLHOOD AMONG GHOSTS.
New York: Knopf, 1976.

Non-Fiction

CHINA MEN. New York: Knopf, 1980.

Articles

"Duck Boy," *New York Times Magazine*, June 12, 1977, 54–55.

"Interview," *Mademoiselle*, 83: 143–149 (March 1977).

"Reservations About China," *MS.*, 7: 67–68 (Oct. 1978).

"San Francisco's Chinatown," *American Heritage*, 30: 36–47 (Dec. 1978).

Janet Lewis

FROM A PUBLIC DIALOGUE BETWEEN LEWIS
AND BRIGITTE CARNOCHAN, GRADUATE STUDENT, U.C. BERKELEY,
OCTOBER 15, 1980, STANFORD UNIVERSITY.

"Being a writer has meant nearly everything to me beyond my marriage and children. It has concerned the way I have thought and the friends I have made. I've noticed that whenever I'm writing, I'm interested in everything, because I'm still waiting for the answer for the next page. I don't pay as much attention, when I'm not writing, to living in general."

With a quiet voice, Janet Lewis began to speak about what it had meant to her to be a writer during a lifetime of more than eighty years. Whenever she gives a public reading or lecture, her audiences span the generations. People who might line up on opposite sides in the arena of sexual politics somehow are moved to share the bleachers and listen to the modest statements of a writer whose gifts are varied, whose subjects are unpretentious, whose voice is gentle, but whose concerns echo their own—how does one find courage and moral equilibrium in a chaotic world? One answer for Lewis is "through writing."

For Lewis, writing is "putting things in order in my head" so as to be able to perceive a situation as completely as possible. This was one of the motivating forces of her novel, *Against a Darkening Sky*, which describes the effect of the encroaching terror of World War II on an ordinary Northern California family. The novel's protagonist, Mary Perrault, opposes the "brute passivity which is the essence of evil and destruction with a renewed moral courage, a courage and morality derived from an old, no longer literally believed in religion, and from a vitality, not entirely physical, which makes her believe in the essential value of life."

Lewis referred to this novel in a wistful way as "rather forgotten and neglected" but true to the experience of living in California, where strength to face life comes partially from the "health and happiness" of the physical climate. Her own appreciation

of California weather issued in part from memories of the harsher
climate of Chicago where she grew up.

Several of Lewis's novels and short stories and many of her
poems reflect her Western experience. For example, the poem she
read to the Stanford audience was "For John Muir, a Century and
More after his Time," written for a centennial celebration in Muir's
honor at Yosemite in 1972. She said that Muir "provided a link" for
her between her early life in the Midwest and her later experience
in the Sierras.

"John Muir first came from Scotland when he was a small boy.
His father settled rather near Madison, Wisconsin, and began
farming—pushing back the wilderness, cutting down trees and
turning the earth. Muir stopped school at that time—the only
schooling he had up to then was grade school in Scotland. It must
have been a very good one because he didn't go to school again until
he went to the University of Wisconsin, and then he just walked
over to the University and said he wanted to come in and they let
him. No application blanks, no examination, no nothing. You all
know, of course, that he is the Father of the Sierra Club and a sort of
patron saint of the moutains."

FOR JOHN MUIR, A CENTURY AND
MORE AFTER HIS TIME

I have seen those Indians in their bunch canoes,
Menominees*, in shallow lake or stream,
Threshing their wild rice. Through Wisconsin haze
I see the water gleam,
                  the small craft tilt,
And through the clustering stems
The small waves lap upon the glacial silt,
As John Muir saw them, years and years ago.
Or do I use
A borrowed memory, learned in my childhood days
From my Ojibway* friends?
                  All that Wisconsin scene,
Familiar as my breath, lives when I choose
To look upon his page:
The muskrat nibbling where the alders bend,
The water plants that gave it summer forage,

Great cumuli piled against thunderous blues
Of summer skies; hepatica and faint anemones
That come before the sunlit woods are leafy;
Bronzed oak and fiery maple, all the gold
Of harvest where the summer ends;
                                   all these
In memory, both mine and borrowed, doubly rich are grown,
Till I can hardly tell his treasure from my own.

Now the Sierra tree, the Sierra wildflower glow
Near polished granite, bright as is the snow
That hoods the mountains of Yosemite
In my remembrance. These I truly know
That I have seen with my own eyes, and yet
There merges with them an unreckoned crowd
Of things more richly seen, of farther heights
Than I have ever traveled; seasons strange
And dangerous moments on that stony range
That Muir was first to call the Range of Light;
Moments of wisdom and intenser sight.
And these I owe to one
Who built his campfire on the canyon rim,
Who woke at dawn, and felt surrounding him
The mind of God in every living thing,
And things unliving, from the snowy ring
Of peaks, to, near his bed, the smallest heather
Lifting a fragile head
                        to greet the sun.

"I began as a poet. Very small-sized too. My first published
poems, or practically the first, were about Indians, about Manibozho
and the legendary Indians of the Ojibways." More than half a
century later, in 1979, with the publication of *The Ancient Ones*,
Lewis returned to the Indian themes of her first poems. In "Awatobi,"
for example, she brings together sites as distant from one another as
the French court of Louis XIV and the battle at Awatobi, united only
in the commonality of bloody violence.

*(Indian tribes.)

Blood in Paris, after the Saint Bartholomew,
Blood at Awatobi, for a cause so similar;
And it was only yesterday. In Time,
Less than three centuries.
Purcell was only lately dead. Racine
Lived almost into the hour of the disaster.
Above the careful gardens of Versailles
Madame de Maintenon and Louis styled the Great
Dreamed of a single faith for France,
And the Huguenots of Nantes
Were fled to England....

Another work that derives from Lewis's familiarity with American Indians is her 1932 novel *The Invasion*, where she recreates the history of the Ojibway Indians around the figure of Neengay, the matriarch of the tribe.

"I thought of Neengay as a great figure, and I loved the stories about her, so when I began to work on the book, I knew that I had to begin with her, rather than with the Irishman who came and married her in 1792. But it wasn't until I was actually working on *The Invasion* that I began to think of her as the matriarch. She became the matriarch as I considered the things she had done."

The female figures in Lewis's fiction and poems are often "cherishers and creators of life," words she has used to describe Mary Perrault in *Against a Darkening Sky*. They are strong women like Neengay with both moral and physical courage. When asked who had provided such a role model in her own life, Lewis answered: "I'm sure the simplest and easiest and truest answer is my mother. She wasn't a matriarch, like Neengay, but she was my role model. She was an enormous help to me all my life, long after she was no longer here in the flesh.

"She wasn't a writer, and she wasn't a painter—my brother was a painter—and she wasn't a musician, although she loved music. But she loved literature; she read poetry with me; she took me to concerts; she saw to it that I got to the opera when I was in my teens; she was a great appreciator and a wonderful survivor. I mean she survived like a weed that springs back after it has been pushed over. My father was a wonderful person, but he was also pretty tempestuous and somehow this never got her down."

If questioned about her attitudes to modern feminism, Lewis is always quick to point out that the drive toward women's liberation did not begin in this decade. Her mother, she said, "was born liberated," and Lewis herself has clearly survived in her roles as wife/mother/writer. She believes that feminism is "a great movement," but adds, "I'm not a campaigner myself, because there isn't enough energy to go around. If I wanted to be a wife, mother, and a writer, there wasn't much left over for campaigning, but I came up in a world in which women were doing very important things. My father was a great friend of Jane Addams, a woman who certainly stepped out and began to change man's world the way it ought to be changed. An aunt of mine was a great friend of the Judge Mary Barthelemew who worked in the juvenile court and who was a wonderful, strong, and compassionate woman. I knew wonderful women doctors here—Dr. Edith Johnson, for instance, an admirable role model for anybody, and Dr. Adelaide Brown, a pioneer obstetrician in San Francisco. Undoubtedly these women found it difficult, but they certainly broke the way."

From general models for life, Lewis turned to the question of literary models. "My father started me out as a writer. My husband kept me going. My father taught English, and any ideas that interested him at the time he also managed to teach as well. I actually had two years working with him at the Lewis institute in a big class in which I sat way in the back and was called 'Miss Lewis' formally every day. For a long time nobody knew we were related— he was very strict with me. He was a novelist and a poet and a wonderful stylist. I think he probably gave me the fundamentals of what I wanted to do. In my father's class we did something which I think is not done very often now. He had a huge class, usually about a hundred, and in the Fall Quarter we wrote daily themes, and they were all corrected.

"Even before I met my husband, Ivor Winters, we had been exchanging poems through the University of Chicago Poetry Club, and his criticism was sensitive and right and never crushing. So we just kept on writing poems and swapping poems after we were married. When we first came to Stanford [where Ivor Winters was to become a leading force in the English Department], I had been ill and my physician had said 'don't type.' This sounds very odd, indeed, but in those days, the whole idea for curing tuberculosis of the lungs was to keep the lungs quiet, and Dr. Brown thought that typing was too much exercise. Anyway, I wrote all my first stories long-hand, and my husband typed them for me, which was a great help. He also read everything I wrote and commented on it, cheered me on."

Other literary influences included nineteenth and twentieth

century French and English writers. "I had majored in French, so that I read a lot of French writing, and if anyone asked me who influenced me or who seemed a wonderful model for style, I would say Flaubert or Henry James or Proust. I loved Colette, but Colette puts me in despair. I can't write like Colette. Anytime I try to write like Colette, I get off my own line."

Speaking of her own work, she admits to a special affection for *Against a Darkening Sky*, which is set in Palo Alto. "It gives you a Palo Alto scene which is not here anymore—the goats we had on Ross Road and Oregon Avenue. It's a scene of impending disaster, before the war, and it's also a scene characteristic of this country in general. There is a great deal of violence in America; we invaded the country to begin with, and it's a pretty violent history, if you stop to look at it. The heroine in the novel, who is a matriarch, came from Scotland, from a settled way of life and a firmer tradition, and she felt very strongly this violence, almost in the earth around her, and its effect on her children."

Ironically, the novel for which she is now best known, *The Wife of Martin Guerre*, went without a publisher for a long time. In describing why she turned to French historical sources for her next novels, Lewis recalled, "I always wanted to get back to France after I had been there in 1920, and so it seemed pleasant to be using a plot that was based in France when I did *The Wife of Martin Guerre*. When it came to choosing another plot, the one for *The Ghost of Monsieur Scarron*, which is about a Paris bookbinder, I'm pretty sure that I chose it largely because I could write about Paris and go back in my imagination, even if I couldn't get back there actually. Eventually I did get back.

"*The Ghost of Monsieur Scarron* might be my best novel. It is longer than the others; it might have more emotional impact if it were shorter, if it had just been trimmed down a little, if there were less history in it. *The Wife of Martin Guerre* goes through very fast and therefore you can figure out what's happening. I hoped *The Ghost of Monsieur Scarron* was going to be my best book, but I'm not sure it is."

When asked how she had found the time to write, while raising two children and caring for a husband and a household of airedales, Lewis's reply was typically straightforward, without a trace of having suffered unduly in her responsibilities: "I put aside a few hours a day. Probably the best hours. My working time has always been when everyone went to school." In one instance she typed the manuscript for a novel with her small daughter sitting on her lap. "She was very small, so I could reach around to the typewriter. I was working on *The Invasion* then, and I was under contract to finish it at a certain time. I worked very regularly, getting up very early in the morning before anybody else, except the baby, who had to be taken care of. She was quiet for awhile; she had her naps, and I knew what I was doing because I had been working on the book for a long time. I knew where I was going and didn't have to pace up and down the floor and say, 'what do I do next?'"

When she spoke of what she *was* going to do next, the list of projects belied her octogenarian status. "Well, besides trying to translate the original French story of Martin Guerre from the book by Jean de Coras, who was one of the actual judges at the trial described in *The Wife of Martin Guerre**, I've been working on a libretto with Alva Henderson called *Mulberry Street*, based on a story by O. Henry. That's been very much fun."

Other libretti include *The Wife of Martin Guerre*, with music by Henry Bergsma; *Birthday of the Infanta*, with Malcolm Seagrave, and *The Last of the Mohicans* with Alva Henderson. "Both Seagrave and Henderson would telephone, play something over the phone, and say 'we want words for this.' Things are easier with Henderson— for one thing, he lives nearby. Since the tape recorder has become a part of our lives, he can sing and record the passages for which he doesn't have the words, and I can play it over and over in peace and quiet and try to fit the words to each note. I don't deserve all of the credit for the libretto of *The Last of the Mohicans*, because Henderson and Robert Darling had sketched out the plan for it before we started working together."

Lewis confirmed that the relationship between writing poetry and libretti is a close one. "The singing ability of the words carries over. One does get the feeling of whether the thing will play or not. I don't mean play musically, I mean whether the action will move the way it ought to and one emotion run into the next, so that the music can carry through from emotion to emotion and build up towards the end. One is very aware of that, and I think that the last one that we are doing together *(Mulberry Street)* is going to play better than any other we've done so far."

Asked if she considered herself a member of any group, Lewis replied: "I'm afraid I don't think of myself as a member of any group. Of course, when I was young, I was a part of the group at the University of Chicago which was called the Poetry Club, and for a little while there was quite a bunch of very interesting people there.

*(See Janet Lewis, "Sources of The Wife of Martin Guerre," *Tri-Quarterly*, Fall, 1982, 104-110.)

I suppose I would have been called one of Ivor Winters's group— I could hardly avoid that. But I don't think of myself as part of any group."

JANET LEWIS, 1899–

Selected Bibliography

Fiction

THE INVASION. New York: Harcourt, Brace, 1932.

THE WIFE OF MARTIN GUERRE. Denver: Swallow Press, 1941.

AGAINST A DARKENING SKY. New York: Doubleday, Doran, 1943.

THE TRIAL OF SOREN QVIST. New York: Doubleday, 1947.

THE GHOST OF MONSIEUR SCARRON. New York: Doubleday, 1959.

Short Stories

GOOD-BYE SON; AND OTHER STORIES. New York: Doubleday, 1946.

Poetry

THE INDIANS IN THE WOODS. Monroe Wheeler Manikin I (series), 1922. 2nd ed., Palo Alto: Matrix Press, 1980.

THE WHEEL IN MIDSUMMER. Lone Gull, 1927.

THE EARTH-BOUND, 1924–1944. Aurora, New York: Wells College Press, 1946.

POEMS, 1924–1944. Denver: Swallow Press, 1950.

THE ANCIENT ONES: POEMS. Portola Valley, Calif.: No Dead Lines Press, 1979.

POEMS OLDS AND NEW: 1918–1978. Denver: Swallow Press, 1981.

Juvenile

THE FRIENDLY ADVENTURE OF OLLIE OSTRICH. New York: Doubleday, 1927.

KEIKO'S BUBBLE. New York: Doubleday, 1961.

Libretti

THE WIFE OF MARTIN GUERRE: AN OPERA IN THREE ACTS. Denver: Swallow Press, 1958.

BIRTHDAY OF THE INFANTA. Los Angeles: Symposium Press, 1981.

Works About the Author

Peck, Ellen McKee. "Exploring the Feminine: A Study of Janet Lewis, Ellen Glasgow, Anaïs Nin and Virginia Woolf," Ph.D. dissertation, Stanford University, 1974.

Joyce Carol Thomas

FROM A PUBLIC DIALOGUE BETWEEN THOMAS
AND DIANE WOOD MIDDLEBROOK, PROFESSOR OF ENGLISH,
STANFORD UNIVERSITY, OCTOBER 25, 1980.

"Born in Oklahoma into a large family, I was the fifth child in a family of nine. One of the things we used to do every fall was to pick cotton, and that involved going to live with other families. The Lightsey family—I used their name in the novel *Marked by Fire*—had twelve children, and we looked forward to living with the Lightseys at harvest time. It was a time to play and spend the night with your best friend. Even though we missed the first part of school because of the necessity of work, we made up for it by telling stories. I suppose we were poor. I *know* we were poor, but there was the joy of being with other children your own age, and telling and hearing stories.

"The central character in *Marked by Fire* is Abyssinia who was born in the state of Oklahoma, where I lived until I was ten. Some of the things that happen to her in the novel happened to me and to some of my girlfriends; so she is a collection of people I knew. I called Abyssinia's mother 'Patience' because that is the noun I think of when I think of my own mother who had a great deal of patience. I introduce Abyssinia in the novel by way of her birth scene in the cotton fields.

THURSDAY MORNING
SEPTEMBER 6, 1951

When Patience awoke, the rooster had not crowed yet. The workers headed for the field just before sunrise. The foreman started a fire down by the bin, using dead wood he had gathered under the spreading trees. For kindling he used slivers of sticks and fallen twigs. The women clustered in a circle around the fire, rubbing their hands together, scanning the field, picking out sets of rows with their eyes. All the while the acrid smoke, lifting itself toward the sky, filled the air and stung the insides of their noses.

31

Then the hungry flame stuck itself to the dried tinder and began eating up the wood. The flame ate and grew taller. When the fire was half as tall as they were, the women fanned out into the field. One by one they knelt down as though worshipping the cotton.

When the sun was a quarter of the way across the sky, Patience tugged the crocus sack back along between the rows to the bin. As the foreman reached for it, she suddenly realized that the bag was the heaviest thing she had ever lifted. Perspiration was beading her nose and soaking her armpits. She felt water running down her legs. Her mind wanted to stop the water, but it would not stop. She could not move; water stuck her to the spot. Water wet her cotton stockings and flooded over the tops of the laced-up shoes and down the dusty trail that the crocus sacks left on their way to the bin.

"Woman!" the foreman shouted at Mother Barker with male uneasiness. This was an area over which he had no authority. "Woman!"

With the urgency in his voice, everybody in the field looked up, their bonnets pushed back from their brows. In the distance Patience saw the women standing like black stalks against the sky.

Mother Barker ran to the weighing-in area. Patience had not moved. One look at Patience's face and it was clear she would never make it back to the cabin in time.

The foreman's wife spoke softly. "Time."

More women came, throwing down their sacks between the fire and the bin, then hurriedly arranging the sacks into a great pallet. Onto this Patience was carefully settled, her legs spread-eagled. The foreman's wife began to hum a song they all knew, a song without words. One of the women took off her bonnet and fanned Patience.

The foreman added more kindling to the fire. His wife placed the water can for drinking over the flame, and soon you could hear the water bubbling under the chorus of the humming.

"Won't be long," the foreman's wife promised.

Soon the humming turned into moaning, and Patience gritted her teeth.

"Wait. Breathe deep, daughter," someone said.

Now and then the humming, the moaning, and the gurgling water mingled until you could not tell where one started and the other stopped.

"Push hard, now."

"Help, mercy!"

The women hummed together like light coming together after the sun has risen noon high while pain and wonder wrapped around each of them in the humming. And the pain sat down on Patience and smothered her.

"Oh, glory."

"Push."

Each woman felt the pain.

"Push."

Each woman felt the pain and wonder as old as time, as old as the sound of the women themselves as they rocked together, humming. Who could push pain away?

"Breathe deep. More deeper."

"Push down. Harder, I say."

The pain crouched low, drew back, and struck Patience so hard that although it was noon, she felt God light the night with lightning and wake up the world with thunder. The pain slashed deeper still until it cut off her breath.

The foreman, bound by a rule as old as human life—that man should not see the mystery of birth for it would be like staring God in the face, left the women and walked toward the grove of blackjack trees. When he reached the grove's edge, he heard his wife say, "Hallelujah!" Then he heard the sound of a slap.

And Abyssinia screamed her way into the world, water on one side, fire on the other.

"Because Abyssinia's birth was attended by the women in the field, they become midwives-in-common at her birth. Each of the women teaches her something different that she needs to know. Some of them teach her about roots, others teach her about storytelling, and later on Abby herself becomes a storyteller and a healer.

"*Marked by Fire* has been categorized by Avon books as young adult fiction. Of course, I wrote it for everyone, but I suppose it is also intended for children of a certain age. I have four children, you know, and I believe that part of my inspiration comes from being around them—from trying to look at things in a childlike way, trying to see the world with their eyes. I tend to be optimistic. And this optimism has meant my survival as a person and as a writer. There is a lot of ugliness in the world I am inclined to ignore a great deal of the time. Children haven't yet come up against the full ugliness of things.

"My children are so much a part of my life. When I was attending grad school at Stanford where I got a masters in education

with an emphasis on Spanish, I used to read my Spanish to them. If I
had a Spanish report to do and was trying to put my kids to sleep, I
would read that to them. So I always try to work them into whatever
I am doing.

"I've always written, for as long as I could hold a pen. My
children, I think, are different. I noticed that when their friends
would come over to visit, these little visitors would intrude a lot,
and while my children intrude too, often they would not bother me.
They would realize I was writing and would go and draw or read, and
leave me alone a great deal. I didn't know how much I had
succeeded in having that happen until other children would visit,
and I realized that their understanding my need for time was all part
of our growing together, through my working and through their
growing up. They just understood and gave me space, but children
are very demanding.

"Now I have just one child at home and it takes a lot of
discipline to have time for him, do my job at San Jose State, and still
have time for my writing. I wake up at about 6:30 in the morning,
get myself bathed and dressed, and send my ten year old off to
school. Then I join a car pool to San Jose State University where I
work as a reading specialist. At San Jose State, and I suppose at most
of our colleges, we have large numbers of students who have
difficulty reading, and one of my jobs is to direct the program which
tests those students, and then I design a reading program that fits a
particular student's needs and work with that student during the
first weeks of the program. From that point on the student generally
can go on his/her own. Sometimes after I finish the morning's work I
have lunch, sometimes I don't, and in the afternoon I sandwich in
some writing. Then at 5:00 I catch my car pool back to Berkeley and
prepare dinner from about 6:45 to 7:45. We have dinner, I help my
son with his homework, listen to him read a little, and then it's
bedtime for him. Sometimes I write, sometimes I read other people's
work, and then I go to bed.

"Before I wrote *Marked by Fire* and my second novel *Bright
Shadow*, which will also be published by Avon, I had published only
poems and written several plays. The volumes of poems, *Bittersweet*, *Crystal Breezes* and *Blessing*, were published by small presses
and are somewhat hard to find now. There is a new collection
coming out called *Inside the Rainbow* that has most of the poems of
the three earlier books in it, along with some new poetry. The plays,
A Song in the Sky, *Look! What a Wonder*, *Magnolia*, and *Ambrosia*,
were performed in San Francisco and Berkeley from 1976-1979. I
once edited the newsletter *Ambrosia* in celebration of Black women.

It was a bimonthly publication of the works of gifted Black women writers.

"Women are central in my writing, and I continue to be supported by women. I recall one woman supporter, the poet Josephine Miles. First she invited me to read with her at Cody's Bookstore a couple of years ago, at which time I read from the manuscript of *Marked by Fire*. A year later she invited me to a Christmas party and asked me what I had done with the novel. I said, 'Oh, it's home in the drawer,' and she said, 'That's a shame, you must really do something with it.' There were some other women writers there and one of them suggested that I send my novel to my present agent Ruth Cohen, and I did. Ruth agreed to represent it and was able to place it with Avon.

"Some of my favorite authors are women writers like Toni Cade Bambara, Lillian Hellman, Virginia Woolf, Maya Angelou, and Josephine Miles. So I continue to be supported by women and in turn see myself as supporting them.

"I have been asked if I am in any sense a feminist or a political writer. I don't start to write to make a political statement. I don't write for that purpose, but obviously everybody makes a statement by choosing what to write about. I guess the title poem in the book called *Blessing*, published in 1974, would qualify as a political poem.

BLESSING

Whereas:
Some stole an entire continent
And never stood trial
I now pronounce you
Not guilty
Of receiving a stolen
Seventy-five dollar suit
Go then
And steal no more
And may what you
Do, say, think
Be a splendid uniform

Whereas:
Some raped a race of women
Then sold their own blood
I now pronounce you

Not guilty
Of non-support and desertion
Go then
And make your daughters
New goddesses and your sons
Young pharaohs

Whereas:
Some bloodied millions
Around the world in the name of
Peace
I now pronounce you
Not guilty
Of stabbing your own brother
Go then
And embrace him

Whereas:
Some supply dope
Uneven exchange for the hopes
They've killed
I now pronounce you
Not guilty
Of selling poison
To the people
Go then
And deal no more

And may your highs
Be a meditated freedom
May you build a brand new earth
And recreate the universe

"In that poem there is the influence of a certain religious tradition—a rhythm and sense of story that probably grew out of my religious background. I grew up in what you would call a fundamentalist Black church and the greatest thing I remember about that church is the music. One of the things expected of the preacher every Sunday is to inspire the congregation and he couldn't do that with just a dry sermon, without any peaks and valleys in it. People had to go away with something. He had to feed them spiritually, and the way he did that was to employ imagery, rhythm and all of that precious language we define as teachers. Of course, he didn't know what they were called, but every good sermon had figurative language in it, and I suppose that made some mark on me.

"My mother was a faithful member of the church. We started getting ready for church on Saturday. Sunday School started at 9:30 and, after a little break, we went back to morning services, which started at 11:00 and continued until 2:00. From 2:00 until 4:00 we had a chance to dash home and eat, but at 6:00—back to church, and often we wouldn't get home until midnight. And if a revival was going on, my goodness, you never got any sleep! And what it did for me was to make me realize by the time I became an adult that I did not want to ever go back to church again. I thought I had had enough to last me. But what I find myself doing often now is returning to hear the music.

"I'd like to read a last poem that says something about the most important influence in my life and writing.

Bittersweet, in memory of my mother:

She
  somersaulted
    into a golden curve

In
  the circle
    was a plague
      of fire

Its arc
  was brilliant
    with anger

And its edges
  hot
    with pain

Out
  of the circle
    I flew

A thistle
   butterfly
      all persimmon

Parched brown
  my hair
     like jetted night

I saw
  the fruit
    lying there

Tempting
  in pain
      and pleasure

More bitter
   than sweet
      Then

Future passed
   through her
     and she was the chrysalis

Who gave me the gift of wings

Quoting from Virginia Woolf, Professor Diane Middlebrook summed up the powerful effect of Joyce Carol Thomas's presence on a public audience:

"Toward the end of *A Room of One's Own*, Virginia Woolf begins thinking about what it will be like in the future when women put into their books what Woolf calls the accumulation of unrecorded life that she can feel all around her. If the woman writer can only learn a way to express it, Woolf says, 'she will light a torch in that vast chamber where nobody has yet been.' That is the feeling one gets from hearing Joyce Carol Thomas read from her works. When she begins to read, we feel that particular kind of happiness settle over us that occurs when you hear someone begin to do something you know you are going to like; you know you're in good hands, and you can hardly wait for what happens next. It seems to me that Joyce has done exactly what Woolf said women would do for us: to light the torch in that vast chamber where nobody had yet been. Her poetry and her prose show us a world that we would not see without her words."

JOYCE CAROL THOMAS, 1938–

Selected Bibliography
Fiction
MARKED BY FIRE. New York: Avon, 1982.
BRIGHT SHADOW. New York: Avon, 1983.
Poetry
BITTERSWEET. Fire Sign Press, 1973.
CRYSTAL BREEZES. Fire Sign Press, 1974.
BLESSING. Jocato, 1975.
INSIDE THE RAINBOW. Palo Alto: Zikawuna Press. 1981
Plays (produced)
A SONG IN THE SKY, 1976
LOOK! WHAT A WONDER!, 1976
MAGNOLIA, 1977.
AMBROSIA, 1978.

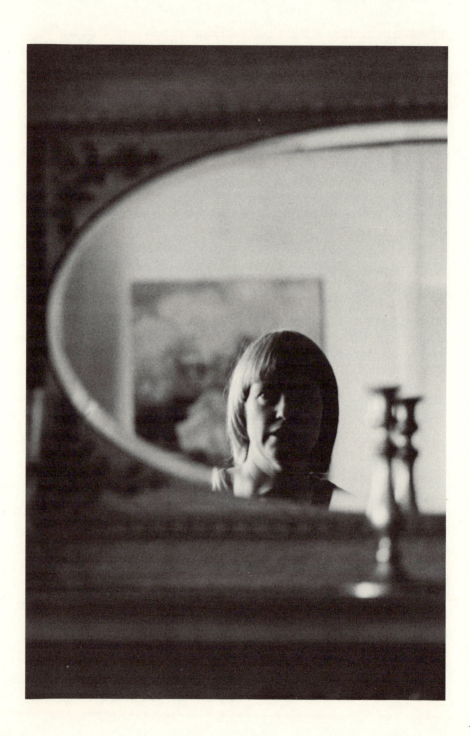

Susan Griffin

FROM A PUBLIC DIALOGUE BETWEEN GRIFFIN
AND NANNERL KEOHANE, PROFESSOR OF POLITICAL SCIENCE,
STANFORD UNIVERSITY, AND CURRENTLY PRESIDENT OF
WELLESLEY COLLEGE, OCTOBER 29, 1980.

Two women, nearly forty, met onstage to exchange ideas culled from their careers as feminist writers and scholars. Their dialogue stretched from the natural world of plants and animals to the realm of phallo-centric culture, establishing global and even cosmic connections. Members of the audience quickly realized that they would have to listen attentively if they were to catch the sophisticated nuances of their discourse.

Commenting on the intersection between woman, nature, and knowledge in Griffin's work, Keohane asked: how can women's knowing of nature be a source of power and positive renewal, as opposed to an excuse for devaluing women, as it has often been in the past?

"We have to change our concept of nature, since we *are* nature," Griffin replied. "All paths lead us back to our own liberation. If we were to try to liberate ourselves as *opposed* to nature, we couldn't achieve that liberation. If we go along with the patriarchal idea of nature, we are going to oppress something inside ourselves."

Griffin described her use of the word "woman," as in the title of her book, *Woman and Nature*. "Although I did mean women specifically, I did not intend to exclude men from the word: I was using 'woman' generically. I am talking about an experience that is human. I said in the beginning of the book that it is men who separate themselves from woman and nature. This is clearly a decision men have made."

Keohane was uncertain about the kind of power that can be derived from an association between women and nature, and a "revolution that begins with the heart."

Griffin's response asked for a redefinition of the way we traditionally think about nature and human experience. "If we redefine nature, we are also redefining our own nature and that

41

includes our emotional nature—that part which has always been called the irrational. Emotion has always been considered something that has to be repressed by thought. If we reconsider this division between thought and emotion, we find it doesn't really exist. What is amusing about the first pages of *Woman and Nature* is that they are satirical restatements of cultural assumptions that have been made from the thirteenth century to contemporary times about what the nature of the universe is. These pages are written in a language that uses such expressions as 'it is said' or 'it has been decided' or 'the truth is clear that.' These statements are always in a passive voice, as if human beings didn't make them. This voice is detached both from a body and from feelings. Yet what I show is that these supposedly detached thoughts were not detached from feelings; they reflect a very deep fear of women and of the earth. In *Woman and Nature*, and in my book on pornography, I tie these fears to a fear of human mortality, a fear of vulnerability, and a fear of change. And underneath this fear is a fear of the knowledge which emanates from our deepest experience connecting matter and spirit."

Keohane commented that when Griffin condemns theorizing "for its detachment, its abstraction or its bloodlessness," as in the beginning of *Woman and Nature*, she is really saying that such theorizing isn't really detached—it just pretends that it is.

"And therefore it turns out to be what is really irrational," Griffin agreed. "It points to the emotions and says that they are irrational, but it's really this posture that is irrational. In fact, it's crazy, it's schizophrenic in the precise definition of that word because it's divided from itself. We have in this culture several institutionalized schizophrenias, one of them being racism, which is tutored into the culture as a way for people to deny all sorts of qualities about themselves and project them onto another person of dark skin and then say 'that person is lazy' and 'that person is very wildly sexual.' This way we can disassociate these parts of ourselves. But it is a mass delusion in which everybody in society agrees to participate, and therefore it doesn't appear to be a madness. Sexism is precisely the same. All the qualities that women are accused of—passivity, wantonness or prudery, both the fear of sex and nymphomania—all of these qualities are human qualities, human possibilities, and they are projected onto a woman. The supposedly theoretical, rational, cool stance is not that at all. It's just a delusionary cover for a whole series of emotions which this culture is afraid to own.

"The only way we ourselves can avoid traps that people in the past fell into when they associated women and emotion is through very deep self-knowledge and by understanding our emotional processes. That is the paradox, and a very beautiful one: we use knowledge and theory and our conceptualizing ability, but we mustn't use them as detached from ourselves and from our emotions. We must use them to *see* these emotions."

Keohane remained skeptical about the human ability to unite reflection and experience. She asked: "If we have this capacity, as human animals, to experience nature in a particular way, which includes reflecting or theorizing on it, aren't we always in danger of separting ourselves from experience?"

Griffin called upon her knowledge of scientific theory and her experience as a mystic. "A very difficult concept for those of us who were raised in this culture is to comprehend the notion of an intelligent emotion, the notion of intelligent or spiritual matter, but in fact there are cultures in which this is the basic assumption, the vision of the universe. I've had many experiences of actual awareness of the knowledge of my body. We in Western culture made a definite decision in the development of our science to detach ourselves from matter. But now science is making discoveries that show us that intelligence is imbedded in matter. What else is DNA? That's an intelligence far superior to any analytical concept we have been able to devise in the past. DNA, this little tiny bit of matter, creates a whole process that we don't even, to this day, begin to understand. Science has also come to certain other conclusions that challenge its own assumptions: for example, Heisenberg's Principle of Uncertainty, where the relationship between the knower and the known turns out to be not so distinct as we thought it was. The knower affects the known.

"Let me give you an example: when Einstein was looking for relativity, he did so because he had an emotional feeling that the universe has unity and sense. He believed this before he discovered the theory of relativity. It was a very strong feeling in him; then he discovered the theory of relativity which proved his feeling. What we're always taught is that a scientist has to be objective and not have any feeling coloring his work, but I don't think that's possible. In Thomas Kuhn's book, *The Structure of Scientific Revolution*, he shows how cultural assumptions have flavored virtually every scientific period and that one sort of paradigmatic discovery then affects all the other supposedly objective theories that arise during that period of time; emotions and feelings always affect the theories we have. The point is not for us to get rid of those emotions but simply to know them for what they are."

In keeping with the focus on Western writers in the CROW dialogues, Keohane asked Griffin what difference it had made that the nature she had experienced had been West Coast, and specifically California nature. Did she think the West Coast setting had influenced her work?

"Yes, I do," Griffin answered. "I became a mystic through writing *Woman and Nature*. I think that the mystical way of viewing the world is aligned to many assumptions that feminist philosophers have begun to adopt. I appreciate being in California. Having been born here, I've received an education that is not so bound in tradition as I would have had in the East. Even the land and the earth here reflect that. There is a lot more wilderness here, and since I was very young, I've had an experience of wilderness that is very accessible. I've spent a lot of time in all the public parks. Until recently, I used to walk on Mount Tamalpais.* There is something very important about locality. In a way, writers become the embodiment of the problem of space and locality because in order to make a living as a writer, one has to relate to New York City. The publishers in New York have certain preconceived notions—for example, they don't believe in 'local' places. They fly about and visit but when they come to a place like San Francisco, they still stay in New York, in a sense, because they stay on the tops of buildings—they don't really understand what happens down here. Even in New York they never hit the streets. There are two New Yorks. New York at the tops of buildings is different from New York in the streets. And 'New York at the tops of buildings' is analogous to what is called the 'universal,' to ideas of 'universality' and 'objectivity.' Actually, universality and objectivity take you out of the universe. The way to really achieve universality, which is to be *of* the universe, is to be very local in your own embodied experience. This is why I feel better in California. When I do theatre or a reading here, I feel part of the community and I'm much happier. I wish the economics of publishing—the fact that a writer has to be published and recognized in New York—didn't exist."

Speaking of her experience as a writer of plays that premiered in California, including the award-winning play *Voices*, Griffin said, "I am very eager to write a play again. I love the theatre and it's taken me years to understand theatre. I don't think that America

---

*(At the time of this dialogue several women hikers had been murdered by an unknown assailant on Mt. Tamalpais.)

particularly understands what theatre is about, and I include myself. In America we've tried to get around language in theatre. We try to recreate the illusion of reality on the stage. But theatre very much comes out of language, it's almost like an active poem, and once I began to understand this, that's how I could write *Voices*. I worked from the language: the characters had ways of speaking about themselves; they wanted very much to talk about themselves, describe their lives. They were all parts of me, but they so much wanted to tell me their stories. Before, when I was younger and writing plays, I made my characters inarticulate in a way that I think we often are in this society. That was a realistic mirror portrait of what goes on in this culture because we are not given a language that really reflects our actual experience.

"In my book *Pornography and Silence* I am led to the conclusion that most of what we call culture (and I'm not talking about the culture of capital C—art, museums, and the like—but culture anthropologically speaking) exists to deny our direct experience rather than to express it. Of course, we can think of exceptions to that, but I believe the rule is that we live in a culture of denial. We don't express our lives, and I feel that the real magic of theatre is opposed to one sort of alienating, tricky illusion or another. The real mask of it is in the expression—that's where you begin and then you can create a spectacle from the expression. But you must begin there. When I empowered my characters and gave them the ability to speak, then suddenly the play became something I was excited about—the language was the real form."

Noting that Griffin has written in many different genres, Keohane asked how she went about deciding which form she would choose at a particular time in her life.

"I don't experience myself as making a decision: I allow the material to find its form. That is, I do experience *trying* to make a decision sometimes and in that case it usually is the wrong decision. When I wrote *Voices* I began it as a novel, and it didn't work as a novel. I would write a few pages and throw them out and write another few pages and throw them out and finally I heard that there was a grant for writing plays at KBSA and I decided what I was writing would make a play. The play started to write itself the minute I had that idea. The work took off. It was the right form. There always seems to be a crisis around the form, however, so when I say that I don't make a decision, that's not quite true. I do decide, but it's not in the way that we usually think of decision-making. You don't sit there and say, 'Now I'm going to decide.' I have to go through a whole process and sometimes it is very painful. It's not just trial and error, it's having to do battle with my own preconceptions.

"Part of this struggle is to get myself to the point where I can trust that it will happen. I find that in the process of writing all the issues of life come up, and the same way that one is anxious, needlessly anxious, about a life situation, one is needlessly anxious about the process of writing. So that I try to make something happen before it is ready to happen or try to be decisive when the decision is already made but I can't see it. You know when it's right because the work begins to come into being. The best metaphor for the process of writing is a garden; when the sprouts come up, you know you're doing the right thing. It's a wonderful feeling; however, I do want to say that it is also painful and murky and difficult. But the wrong path is also valuable—it's a stage in the development. You learn a great deal from writing and one of the things you learn is that there are difficulties and one gets through them.

"Tillie Olsen has written extensively about silences in writers' lives that have been imposed on the life and particularly on women's lives, and I also write about that a great deal. But then there is another kind of silence that is self-imposed, in which the part of you that is an ally to the repressive influence of culture silences yourself, so that often I will go through a period of silence when there is something I'm not wanting to face. Then there is also the natural process where something sleeping is coming to maturation. There are so many different kinds of silence.

"When I chose the title *Pornography and Silence* I was using silence in a pejorative sense—I was talking about the generation of silence and woman's experience: invisible, *hidden.* I think of the repression of certain events from woman's history such as the fact that Sappho's writings were burnt, that Kate Chopin's wonderful turn-of-the-century novel fell out of print for years and years. There is also the fact that women receive something like one-sixteenth of the various grants like Guggenheims and Rockefellers that enable people to write. In the feminist community we're aware of these facts. But at the deeper level, which we haven't begun to comprehend, is the great psychological damage done to us by centuries and centuries of silence regarding women's lives, not only the silencing of women's creative abilities, but a silence about us. This sometimes feels as if it were conspiratorial, but in fact it is not. The most disturbing silence concerns women's daily experience. I believe that this silence works hand in hand with pornography. Real portraits of women have not been projected through this culture. For instance, the real portrait of a mother, who is a woman who has to be extremely intelligent and canny and witty and physically strong to deal with children. Children are physically heavy. We think of mothers as beings who have to be protected, who are madonna-like and serene all the time; nobody can mother a child and remain like that. You get dirty and sweaty. You have to lift them and yell at them. Since the real canniness and intelligence and other qualities in women are never portrayed in the culture, you have instead a blank screen onto which pornographic images of women are projected. If the real image existed, the pornographic image would not be so effective, but it's all we see. And then what happens is that this pornographic image starts to become real because a little girl growing up in this society has no access to the real experience of her mother or other women—she doesn't inherit any language that gives her access to her own experience. She learns that in order to function in society effectively, even to be recognized in social circles, she herself has to try to project an image of the pornographic woman. She has to impersonate pornographic ideas of a woman. I don't mean that she has to go slinking around in a pornographic model's costume, but I'm including in pornography the idea that woman is submissive; that she is pretty but dumb; that she likes to be dominated; that she's an object for somebody's pleasure; that she likes to serve."

Keohane moved from this theme of the young girl who learns about herself from inauthentic images to the theme of dialogue in general. She recalled Griffin's statement that she writes in response to interior voices. Keohane asked if Griffin gradually filtered out the bad voices and retained only the dialogues with voices she regarded as wholesome.

"I don't think you could honestly say that you just have dialogues with voices you regard as wholesome. I don't see how anyone born in this culture can not have these conflicts, which are generated from basic human conflicts, but then this culture shapes them and makes them worse, rather than mediating them and helping us go through certain conflicts with nature. This culture teaches us to be more and more alienated from nature and to live in a detached way from nature. All of us, even if we are feminists or politically enlightened, have this dialogue going on in our heads all the time, every moment, and I think it is extremely important for people in a political movement to be psychologically very sophisticated. We have such a powerful, potentially powerful, movement, particularly if we were to put together the movement of people of color and the ecology movement and the feminist movement. There is no reason why we have to sit back and allow nuclear weapons to be proliferated or allow girl children or black children to be mistreated in any school system. We don't have to allow this to continue. I think the reason that we don't have our full power now is because we stop ourselves. I'm not saying that there aren't real circumstances, that there isn't a real fascist movement in this country that would like to silence us, but we have much more power than that particular movement. The reason we don't win all the time against those forces is because we undermine ourselves. This is an age in which we've been given a deeper understanding of the mind, in part because of the work of such as Freud and Reich. Of course, Freud was a man very influenced by the sexism of his age, and we can't take him whole cloth for that reason, but we have to use his knowledge and integrate it into our political understanding and into our own lives, so that we change ourselves, because otherwise we're going to continue fighting and undermining each other."

Keohane felt that Griffin's work had explored the most central arena in contemporary feminist thought, that terrain where knowledge and power and nature come together, and she asked Griffin to read a poem called "Deer Skull" that expressed these concerns. Griffin said that "Deer Skull" came from an unpublished trilogy called *Knowledge*. "Among other things it is an investigation of a different kind of knowledge accessible to all of us, yet one we resist all the time, though it is knowledge that holds incredible power and joy."

DEER SKULL

1.
I keep placing my hands over
my face, the finger tips just
resting on the place where I feel
my eyebrows and the fine end
of a bone. My eyes are covered
with the blood of my hands, my
palms hold
my jaws. I do this at dinner
my daughter says

Are you alright
and by a common miracle
when I smile
she knows I am.

2.

I ask her what she will do
after we eat. Sleep she
tells me. But I will clean
the deer skull, wash it.

3.

You gave me this skull in the woods
told me to bring it clean
and tell the story I had told you
before, about how the deer had
come to me, and I said I would.

4.

And I put this skull on an old
newspaper, pulled the lower part
of the jaws free, touched it first
carefully, as if it would fall apart
in my hands, the bone paper
thin, and then I saw I could
scrub, so brushed the surface with
steel and my fingers and more
and more this surface became
familiar to me.

5.

I wanted to see the lines of it
what it would be if it had been
polished by the wind, the water
and my hands this agent making
the skull more itself.
Slowly I was not afraid at all
and my fingers went into the deepest
holes of this thing, not afraid

for myself or it, feeling
suddenly as if my cleaning this
small fragment of earth away
from the crevices inside was
like loving.

    6.

But it was then I touched the place
where the eyes were that I knew
this was the shell of the deer that had
lived here, this was this deer
and not this deer, her home and
now empty of her, but not
empty of her, I knew also, not
empty of her, as my hands
trembled.

    7.

And in that instant remembered you
had been in that body of
that deer dying, what
does it feel like to be a deer
dying, the death consumes
you like birth, you are
nowhere else but in the center.

    8.

Remembering those gentle deer
that watched me as I wept,
or the deer that leapt as if
out of my mind, when I saw
speaking there in that green place
the authority of the heart,
and the deer of the woods where
my feel stood stared at me until
I whispered to her and cried
at her presence.

9.

And when I cleaned the skull
I washed myself and sat
my body half out of the water
and put my hands again over
my face, my fingers edging the
bone over my eyes, and I thought
how good this feels and this
is a gesture you make.

10.

Tell this story of the deer's skull
you asked gently and so I
came in my own time to put
these words carefully here
slowly listing each motion
on this thin paper
as fragile and as tough
as knowledge.

Questions from the audience sparked a new dialogue between those seated in the auditorium and the poet on the platform.

ON THE UNION OF EMOTION AND LOGIC...

"The fact that I was a poet enabled me to write *Woman and Nature*. I did as much as I could over four years. I educated myself in the history of science and became more interested in it than I had ever been, but I always approached it as a poet. I went through incredible experiences; for instance, I went through a feeling of terror. I was afraid to challenge the notions of Newton, the fathers, the authorities, afraid to challenge the assumptions of science. I thought I should have twenty or thirty more years of education or a doctorate degree to make me an authority before I should presume to do this, and I realized at a certain point that the ignorance and fear I felt was real; it could even be a strength if I gave expression to it. I wrote a section in the book called 'Plutonium' which expresses all of our feelings of powerlessness before the awesome state of knowledge that science possesses, and throughout the writing of the book, I express the ironic situation of a human being who feels that the ability to control her own life has been taken away from her and that there are experts who claim they know more about her own body and her own life than she does. And this also led to the invention of the voices and authorities in the book. I think we create those voices of authority out of our fear of the power of nature; we create them and then we are afraid of them. As a writer, I constantly work with my own emotions and I find that my emotional process reflects whatever I am writing. During *Woman and Nature* the voices I was afraid of challenging existed within me as a patriarchal voice. That voice was telling me 'you're crazy,' 'you're not the right person to be writing this book.' So there were two people all the time in me, two people in the dialogue, Woman and Nature on one side and patriarchal science on the other."

ON WRITER'S BLOCK...

"I had a period where there was a problem in my life I didn't want to face. For many reasons I was not publicly a lesbian, and so even though my friends knew I was a lesbian, I didn't want to write about it. When I did write about it, when I decided not to hide that fact publicly any more, a lot of poetry out of that experience suddenly appeared. There are many reasons for dry periods. They can be looked at as symptoms; for instance, if you have a headache, in a way you're glad you have a headache, because if there is something wrong in your body, you want to know about it. For a writer, the dry period is a symptom that there is something in your life you're not allowing to come to expression; you're not confronting it and it's doing you damage. It should be looked at as something that can help you, and not as an enemy."

ON SELF-KNOWLEDGE AND CULTURAL CHANGE...

"For me, self-knowledge could only begin because there was a feminist movement. I was part of the feminist movement in the very beginning. I think we have to re-examine the idea of cause and effect, which is more complicated than Western science has presumed it to be. Definitely there is causality in the world, but there is also synchronicity. I believe that the universe is one fabric and you can start in many different places on the fabric to move to a truth, but there is a ripple effect. If I begin to become self-knowledgeable, I'm going to be led to question cultural assumptions.

If I start to question cultural assumptions, I'm going to have to look at *myself* at some point."

ON THE DENIAL OF EXPERIENCE...

"I wrote for about a year on *Pornography and Silence* and it seemed to me fairly good writing, but I wasn't terribly excited about it. Then I wrote what seemed to me to be an essential chapter on the subject of sadomasochism. I had been trying to avoid writing about that because I find sadomasochism repulsive and horrifying, and so naturally I didn't want to write about it, particularly since when you write about something, you always find traces of it in yourself. That was a great exercise in avoidance. When I began to write that chapter, what I discovered was so important that I threw everything else out and had to rewrite the book all over again.

"And I had some synchronistic experiences while I was trying not to face that material. I was being judgmental towards people who suffer from sado-masochistic compulsions, which is not to say that I approve of that behavior now. In addition, I had two experiences with animals dying around me—a frog died in a hot tub and a bird died in my house. The gist of all this was that I had to take them out of the house, and when I took the frog out of the hot tub, I felt horrible and didn't want to look at it. But by the time of the bird, I had matured, and I looked at the bird just as I threw it away. Suddenly my heart went out to this bird and I realized, if you're going to be afraid to look at something and be repelled by it and allow yourself to be controlled by it, then the experience you have is going to be horrible, but if you will look on it, really look on it, and allow yourself to resonate with it, it will be an experience you're glad to have. Even though it's sorrow, I'm glad to have experienced that kind of compassion."

ON FREUD AND FATE...

"Sometimes I just sit in my library when I'm caught in a thought and ask, 'Which book shall I read?' and one of them comes out to me. This happened with Freud. I looked at an essay where Freud talks about fate, and for the first time in my life, reading Freud about fate, I understood what that word meant. I think most of us, when we were in school, read Greek tragedy and were taught how important fate was to the Greeks. We were also taught that modern Western culture is not so concerned with fate, and we couldn't really understand what they meant by the word fate. Suddenly it struck me: I know what fate means. Fate means nature. Nature's power to control us and the fact *that we are nature* is our fate. That is the human condition: death, vulnerability, the fact that we begin as infants lying in bed wanting food. That led me to reinterpret the Oedipus myth, which Freud uses, and I went back to where he talks about Oedipus in another piece of writing. I looked at the tragedy and the legend and realized that Freud's interpretation of the Oedipus myth is a literal interpretation. Freud usually takes things as symbolic, but when he gets to the child wanting to sleep with his mother, he says the tragedy of Oedipus is about Oedipus wanting to sleep with his mother, which is very literal. Then I realized that it wasn't so much that Oedipus wanted to make love with his mother, but rather that Oedipus wanted the *knowledge* of the mother. In this culture there is a warfare between two kinds of knowledge, knowledge of culture and knowledge of the body, and it's interesting that carnal knowledge has a double meaning. Eros and knowledge are very wrapped up with each other. You can't really have an erotic experience without knowing. Part of your desire for Eros is to know another—the erotic movement towards the mother is to know her. The relationship with the mother is where we hook up woman and nature in the beginning because it is the mother who has so much power over our lives. She can leave us there to starve in the crib or change our diaper and feed us. Mortality and vulnerability are first in the body, experienced in relation to this woman. There is a wonderful book on this subject, *The Mermaid and the Minotaur* by Dorothy Dinnerstein. It seemed to me that Oedipus, in wanting to sleep with his mother, wanted that knowledge. He wanted that bodily knowledge, but his father represented a denial of that knowledge. His father represented culture—not all culture, since there can be a culture that reflects that knowledge of the body or the knowledge we associate with mothers, but what made Oedipus a tragedy was that his father's culture couldn't reflect carnal knowledge because it made a decision to be afraid of nature—to deny nature's power. And that was why Laius decided to murder Oedipus, his own son, because he was told that his son would mean his own death. Well, that is always true; our children are reminders to us that we are going to die. As they grow up, we grow old and put one foot in the grave. The knowledge of our own mortality, which is our natural condition, is what this culture tries to deny and cannot forgive."

SUSAN GRIFFIN, 1943–

Selected Bibliography
Poetry
DEAR SKY. Berkeley: Shameless Hussy Press, 1971.
LIKE THE IRIS OF AN EYE. New York: Harper and Row, 1976.
Non-Fiction
WOMAN AND NATURE: THE ROARING INSIDE HER. New York: Harper and Row, 1978.
RAPE, THE POWER OF CONSCIOUSNESS. New York: Harper and Row, 1979.
PORNOGRAPHY AND SILENCE: CULTURE'S REVOLT AGAINST NATURE. New York: Harper and Row, 1981.
MADE FROM THIS EARTH: AN ANTHOLOGY OF WRITINGS. New York: Harper and Row, 1983.
LET THEM BE SAID. Mama Press, 1973.
LETTERS. Twowindows Press, 1973.
THE SINK. Berkeley: Shameless Hussy Press, 1973.
Plays
VOICES: A PLAY FOR WOMEN. New York: Feminist Press, 1975.
Anthologies
Ellen Bass and Florence Howe, eds. NO MORE MASKS! New York: Doubleday, 1973.
WOMEN: FEMINIST STORIES BY NEW FICTION AUTHORS. New York: Eakins, 1971.

Tillie Olsen

FROM A PUBLIC DIALOGUE BETWEEN OLSEN AND
MARILYN YALOM, STANFORD CENTER FOR RESEARCH ON WOMEN,
NOVEMBER 5, 1980 AND SUBSEQUENTLY.

Tillie Olsen is best known as the author of a collection of short stories named for its title piece *Tell Me a Riddle*, of an unfinished novel entitled *Yonnondio: From the Thirties* and of a book on the forces that impede literary creativity, appropriately entitled *Silences*. Since 1961 when "Tell Me a Riddle" received the O. Henry Prize, her books have acquired a large national and international readership who admire, almost to the point of reverence, the compact richness of her art and the emotive force of her person.

Olsen writes about people whose lives are circumscribed by their class and their sex. Yet she cannot be narrowly categorized as a "working class" or a "feminist" writer, since her work presses upon such broad social and existential issues as the interrelationship of self, family, and community, and the brute fact of death.

Born Tillie Lerner in Nebraska in 1912, she was the daughter of Jewish-Russian immigrants. As in her autobiographical novel *Yonnondio*, her father worked on a farm, in a packinghouse and in a number of other settings in an effort to improve his family's economically marginal situation. Having grown up with five siblings and committed socialist parents, Tillie developed a working-class consciousness at an early age—a consciousness made more acute when she crossed the tracks to the academic high school in Omaha, Nebraska, and "felt the wounds of being of a different class." Yet she was able to find in books "a special refuge and a special resource" that remained with her throughout life.

The future writer did not finish high school. Having completed the eleventh grade, Olsen reminds us that she did better than most of her generation where few got beyond the eighth grade. She became, like her parents, committed to social action and retrospectively considers the political climate of the thirties as one of the "special factors" that helped to orient her adult life. In the late twenties and early thirties, she was a member of the Young Communist League, which was comparable, in Olsen's opinion, to being involved in the anti-war movement of the sixties. During this period, she subordinated her desire to write fiction and poetry to her participation in political work, and, even more crucially, to her need to earn a living.

Ironically, it was out of her imprisonment for trying to organize packinghouse workers in Kansas City that she was able to begin her first novel, *Yonnondio.* "I spent some time in Kansas City in the Argentine jail, where I developed first pleurisy, then incipient T.B. It meant I had to be taken care of, was given thinking-writing time. I began *Yonnondio* the same month that I became pregnant." These circumstances led to the birth of Olsen's first daughter, when she was nineteen. In 1933, she moved to California, first to Stockton and then to San Francisco. By 1935 when she attended the American Writers Congress in the company of such luminaries as Malcolm Cowley and Ford Madox Ford, she had already made a name for herself in leftist intellectual circles as a contributor to the newly founded *Partisan Review* and the *New Republic. Partisan Review* published three of her pieces in 1934, including "The Iron Throat" taken from the first chapter of *Yonnondio.* In 1936, she began her liaison with the union organizer Jack Olsen, who was to become the father of her four other daughters. As a working mother, Olsen raised five children, was active in a wide array of social and political causes ranging from the CIO to the PTA, and shared a complex, difficult, rewarding family life that is perhaps best glimpsed in two of the *Tell Me a Riddle* stories—"Hey Sailor, What Ship?" and "Oh Yes."

Olsen's return to the publishing of fiction after an interval of more than twenty years was occasioned by the receipt of a Stegner Fellowship in Creative Writing at Stanford University in 1956. In the fifties, she wrote the four *Tell Me a Riddle* stories which appeared collectively in 1962. Then, with the unexpected discovery of the manuscript of her first novel, considered lost for many years, Olsen published in 1974 a still-unfinished version of *Yonnondio: From the Thirties,* a work that recalls the naturalism of Zola and the style of Elizabeth Madox Robert's *Time of Man* without losing its distinctly personal mode of literary expressionism. Her long-awaited last book, *Silences,* 1978, originally conceived as a talk to the Radcliffe Institute where she was a fellow from 1962-1964, received enthusiastic critical acclaim from reviewers who signaled its exhaustive scholarship and original style. In it, Olsen explodes the myth that genius "will out" whether it resides in a garret room or a manor house. Instead, she presents a convincing case for the influence of external circumstances on human achievement, most notably on the achievement of women whose literary productivity has traditionally been curtailed not only by material conditions but also by the demands of motherhood and the role of social nurturer.

To a large extent, Olsen understands her own success and limitations as a writer within this same conceptual framework. She sees herself as having been inhibited from writing by the general circumstances shared by most women whose lives are consumed by paid work and family responsibilities. As she writes in *Silences*: "substantial creative work demands time," and time was the least available commodity for Olsen when she "raised children without household help" and "worked on everyday jobs as well." If she was able to publish her first book at fifty, it was partially because at that time of life her hands were "lightened" by the exodus of children from the home.

Olsen insists that whenever a person achieves public recognition as a creator, "it is not by virtue of great innate capacity, which is far more common than has been assumed...but by virtue of special, freaky luck." She traces her own luck to the historical accident of having come to politics and publishing in the thirties when American literature began to concern itself seriously with the experience of people from the working class, and when there was a place to be published in many new little magazines. Olsen sees a parallel between the intellectual climate of the thirties, which encouraged her writing, and the civil rights and women's movements of the sixties and seventies, which created an audience for the writing of blacks and women.

She is, nonetheless, wary of such labels as "women's" literature, "black" literature, and "working class" literature. Such terms tend to be patronizing and exclusionary, and deny the universality of experience rooted in class, race and gender. Olsen says of herself that she writes about "people who must work for a living—that is, most of humanity. 'Working class' sounds limited, alien, 'them out there.'"

Class, gender and race are the three major factors which, according to Olsen, influence a person's sense of self. In 1978, in a Stanford course called "Sense of Identity in Modern Women Writers" where Olsen spoke as a guest lecturer, she surprised the students by asserting that for most human beings, sex, class and color create one's sense of identity. Two years later in a public speech at Stanford, she elaborated upon this point: "When I grew up...quest for identity was something only privileged people could concern themselves with." She believes that our core sense of identity is generally so "largely circumstanced by our sex, class and color" that the influence of other personal and cultural factors is of secondary importance.

Here as elsewhere Olsen chooses to veer away from strictly psychological issues, although her writing reveals a fine attention to the nuances of interpersonal process and an ability to create psychologically credible characters. Rather than focus on the "self" as a sui-generis entity, she conceptualizes quest for identity as a profound freedom issue with a societal base. Her convictions seem to spring both from a Marxist and feminist understanding of the material conditions that shape people's lives, and from her personal experience as a woman who stood there ironing, listening, nursing, fully immersed in the elemental issues of life.

Despite the generally insurmountable difficulties creative women face—and these are eloquently outlined in *Silences*—being a woman has not been for Tillie Olsen, as it was for Sylvia Plath, an "awful tragedy." [Plath, *Journals*.] The twenty years spent bearing and rearing her children, when "the simplest circumstances for creation did not exist," did not succeed in destroying Olsen's spirit or extinguishing her hope to write. She carried literature with her from home to the workplace, a poem tacked to the refrigerator door, a book held open in one hand while the other hung onto a bus strap. She kept her writing alive "after the kids were in bed, after the household tasks were done." And as she nurtured her children, so her life as a woman/mother/housekeeper nurtured her literary output. Much of her writing is anchored in the recognizably female experience of sustaining human life, from the basic physical care of babies and dying people to the encouragement of adolescents and young adults seeking their autonomy.

Olsen attends to subjects which male authors would usually ignore or find trivial: ironing, vacuuming, "bacon and eggs in the icebox." Her works are written from a distinctly female, often feminist, point of view, which underscores women's disadvantaged position in a society based on male values and privileges, without losing compassion for the victimized male as well as the victimized female. She was one of the first in the past quarter century to bring a consciously gendered voice to literature. That voice did not go unnoticed by members of the women's movement who recognized in Olsen a precursor and role model for their own literary endeavors. Olsen would be the first to attribute her publication success and literary renown in the seventies to the "luck" of having found a responsive audience in the feminist community. As she writes in

Silences: "fortunate...are those born into the better climates, when a movement has created a special interest in one's sex, or in one's special subject."

It is largely her style, however, which accounts for her prestige in literary circles. Her style has evolved from the dense richness of *Yonnondio* to the compact lyricism of *Tell Me a Riddle* to the almost elliptical prose of *Silences*, retaining throughout a distinctive poetic quality. For example, in *Yonnondio* the description of work in a Chicago packinghouse during the summer months rises rhythmically with the heat to an unbearable crescendo, fusing the inhuman and the human—factory and workers—into a massive, suffering organic whole.

> And now the dog days are here, the white fierce heat throbbing, when breathing is the drawing in of a scorching flame and the pavement on the bare feet of the children is a sear; when the very young and the very old sicken and die, and the stench cooking down into the pavements and the oven houses throbs like a great wave of vomit in the air.
>
> There in the packing houses the men and women somehow toil through. Standing there, the one motion all day, their clothes salty with sweat, or walking in and out of the cooler till the cold is a fever and the heat a chill, and the stink bellying up from the blood house and casings forces the beginning of a vomit, even on those who boasted they hadn't a smeller any more.
>
> Oh yes, the heavy air clamps down like a coffin lid over the throbbing streets, on the thin cries of babies and the querulous voices of the old, and a sound of breathing hoarse and strained, of breathing feeble and labored goes up; and from beneath the glisten of sweat on a thousand brows, a mocking bitterness in old old words: is it hot enough for you? in a dozen dialects, is it hot enough, hot enough, hot enough for you?

Although the world depicted by Olsen in most of her writing is a world of material marginality and social conflict, and sometimes—as in *Yonnondio*—the bleakness rises to a level of almost malevolent intensity, still the characters in her fiction do not fall into despair. When asked what redeems her characters and keeps them from permanently despairing, Olsen articulates her belief in the power of human resiliency, as illustrated both in personal efforts at change and in the various liberation movements throughout history.

The human baby is one of her favorite examples of the

potential for boundless possibility born within each person, which becomes undermined all too soon by the "color of our skin, the sex of our body, our walk of life," and other social and historical factors. Baby Bess in *Yonnondio*:

> Bess who has been fingering a fruit jar lid absently, heedlessly drops it, aimlessly groping across the table, reclaims it again. Lightning in her brain. She releases, grabs, releases, grabs. I can do. Bang! I did that. I can do I! A look of a neanderthal concentration is on her face. That noise! In triumphant, astounded joy she clashes the lid down. Bang, slam, whack. Release, grab, slam, bang, bang. Centuries of human drive work in her; human ecstacy of achievement; satisfaction deeper and more fundamental than sex. I can do, I use my powers; I!

At the other end of the life cycle are those who have been maimed and deformed—the aged and the dying—as portrayed in Olsen's masterpiece "Tell Me a Riddle." Nowhere is her art more evident than in this fifty-four page novella, the story of a poor, elderly, querulous Jewish couple, married for forty-seven trying years, and ultimately faced with the wife's cancerous death. In its compassionate evocation of one woman's encounter with death, "Tell Me a Riddle" has been compared to Tolstoy's classic story, "The Death of Ivan Ilych." What distinguishes "Tell Me a Riddle" from most other works on this subject is its focus on the couple as a unit experiencing death together. Even such a couple as this one, with its bitter history of antagonistic personalities and desires, can, when death becomes imminent, rise to a level of silent understanding that gives dignity to their final moments together. The story's special poignancy derives largely from the character of husband and wife. They are not conventional tragic figures from the world of a Hemingway or a Malraux, going to their deaths gravely with a sense of accomplishment. They are simply two people from the everyday world, undistinguished, even comical; two people who have known hardship, poverty, unpleasantness, the hourly grind of work and family life. They come from Olsen's world and represent not only its modest economic level and social class, but also the ability of its members to care for one another through a lifetime accumulation of mutually inflicted scars.

The mix of insults and idealism, the stylized Jewish accents that have both a particular and universal ring, the movement from outer conversation to inner dialogue—all contribute to an inimitable literary texture. The husband waits out his wife's death talking to himself in the familiar ironic, name-calling fashion of their married years, while she sings bits of songs and recites political credoes from an earlier life in Russia, when, as a girl, she was moved to revolutionary action by the vision of a better life to come.

> "Aah, Mrs. Miserable," he said, as if she could hear, "all your life working, and now in bed you lie, servants to tend, you do not even need to call to be tended, and still you work. Such hard work it is to die? Such hard work?"
> The body threshed, her hand clung in his. A melody, ghost-thin, hovered on her lips,. . . .
>> *No man one except through others*
>> *Strong with the not yet in the now*
>> *Dogma dead war dead one country*
> "It helps, Mrs. Philosopher, words from books? It helps?"

Inspired by the socialist ideals of "two of that generation," Olsen never forgets the "not yet in the now." Unlike certain other writers from the American and French realistic traditions, Flaubert for example, who "whenever he saw a human being. . .saw them as they would be as a corpse," Olsen is always concerned with the human potential for transcendance. She says of herself: "I am one of those writers who, in Emily Dickinson's words, 'dwell in possibility, a fairer house than prose.'"

As one critic wrote almost ten years ago in *Ms Magazine*, Olsen allows no split between her art and her humanity. She sees her style as inseparable from the ideas and emotions it must convey; style consists of saying "what needs to be said in the best way possible. But it is the subject matter, the 'what needs to be said,' that creates the 'style.'" Olsen thinks of herself primarily as "an oral/aural writer." When she writes, she reads it aloud to make certain that it sounds right to her ear. "Every sentence, every paragraph has to do so damned much work; trying to get everything said including that which is not on the page: the silences between sentences, the selection of detail that conveys the most, the sentence or two of dialogue that characterize.

"I use the 'mother tongue' primarily, the language of the deepest, purest emotion, language that does not come primarily out of books, but the language of first thought, emotion. As Blake said, and I do quote this over and over—'a tear is an intellectual thing.' To move people to comprehension, the tear, the emotion, which includes the intellect, must be present, first of all in the writer, then in the work, then in the reader. The work of 'style' for me has also to do with the understanding, then the selection out of my vast freightage of material—accumulated over years and still accumulating. Then the struggle for the words, the rhythm. As I express that which is not being said enough or said at all, that creates an additional pressure on style. To try to say that differently: when one's vision is an opposing vision to the dominant one, as it continues to be for those of us who are feminist or/and writers of color or/and write with a working class sense, whether we realize it or not, these affect how we write.

"There is something else that I learned early, and everything in my life reinforced: don't have contempt for people, don't have contempt for your readers, trust them, they are intelligent, they have lived as profoundly as you have. Maybe they haven't articulated what you the writer have, but they'll fill it in with their own lives, they'll write it along with you. You do not have to spell it out for them. You do not have to tell them everything. You do not have to, in that particular kind of protective way, bring them into your imagined world. They will bring to it their full beings, they'll give your writing a dimension it may not really have on the page, and I assure you I am not as good a writer as some of you may think I am. It is you and what you bring to it...the common work that we do together...all this is part of the making of style."

When Olsen speaks in public, despite her occasional stuttering and a tendency to amplify a central theme almost to the point of digression, she has a remarkable ability to capture and hold an audience. She knows how to speak directly to an individual in the crowd and, at the same time, to create a sense of human community within the group. This is due, in part, to her compelling voice, but perhaps even more to the intensity of her emotions, her convictions, and her sense of authority, as she circles back, incessantly, to the interlocking themes of human endurance, resistance, and beneficent action.

She is fond of reading aloud from "I Stand Here Ironing" passages that embody these themes. The story, drawn from the experiences of her eldest child, suggests the affectionate interplay between a mother and daughter for whom life has not been easy, as well as the more hostile interplay between family and outside world. "I Stand Here Ironing" begins and ends with the image of mother at the ironing board (like Whistler's mother forever in a rocker) fretfully hoping that her nineteen year old will somehow find the strength to resist those oppressive forces which would roll over her, like an iron over a dress.

She starts up the stairs to bed. "Don't get *me* up with the rest in the morning." "But I thought you were having midterms." "Oh, those," she comes back in, kisses me, and says quite lightly, "in a couple of years when we'll all be atom-dead they won't matter a bit."

She has said it before. She *believes* it. But because I have been dredging the past, and all that compounds a human being is so heavy and meaningful in me, I cannot endure it tonight.... She has much to her and probably little will come of it. She is a child of her age, of depression, of war, of fear.

Let her be. So all that is in her will not bloom—but in how many does it? There is still enough left to live by. Only help her to know—help make it so there is a cause for her to know—that she is more than this dress on the ironing board, helpless before the iron.

Wherever Olsen goes, her impact on the public is tremendous. Her voice sweeps across an audience like the waves of an ocean, sometimes repetitious but never monotonous, carrying her listeners along into an exploration of life, literature, and, above all, the necessity of human solidarity and resistance in the face of social injustice. Often in her talks and readings, she herself is brought to tears by a passionate sense of responsibility to her formerly silenced self and to all the silenced people for whom she bears witness. Unsolicited letters attest to her sway. They speak of feelings "too deep for words," of "tears that come unexpectedly." One of the most telling statements was found in a single sentence: "Tillie has given us back to ourselves."

TILLIE OLSEN, 1912–

Selected Bibliography

Fiction

TELL ME A RIDDLE. Philadelphia: J.P. Lippincott, 1961. (now in Delacorte, Delta, Laurel, Dell editions).

"Requa," in BEST AMERICAN SHORT STORIES OF 1971. Boston and New York: Houghton Mifflin, 1971.

YONNONDIO: FROM THE THIRTIES. New York: Delacorte Press/ Seymore Lawrence, 1974. (Also Delta, Laurel editions).

Non-Fiction

SILENCES. New York: Delacorte Press/Seymore Lawrence, 1978.

Rebecca Harding Davis. LIFE IN THE IRON MILLS. New York: Feminist Press, 1972. Biographical interpretation by Tillie Olsen.

Works About the Author

O'Connor, William Van. "The Short Stories of Tillie Olsen." *Studies in Short Fiction*, 1(Fall 1963), 21–25.

Boucher, Sandy, "Tillie Olsen: The Weight of Things Unsaid." *Ms*, September 1974, 26–30.

Anon. "Tillie Olsen." *The Dictionary of Literary Biography*, 1980, 290–297.

Rosenfelt, Deborah. "From the Thirties: Tillie Olsen and the Radical Tradition." *Feminist Studies* Vol. 7, No. 3 (Fall 1981) 371–406.

Ursula LeGuin

FROM A PUBLIC DIALOGUE BETWEEN LEGUIN
AND ANNE MELLOR, PROFESSOR OF ENGLISH,
STANFORD UNIVERSITY, NOVEMBER 6, 1980.

Ursula LeGuin is a distinguished writer of science fiction, the only woman who has thus far been recognized as a master of the genre. Her audience includes readers of various nationalities and children of all ages, for whom *The Earth Sea Trilogy* and *The Beginning Place* are memorable landmarks in the world of fantasy. Her sizeable audience at Stanford, sprinkled with a large number of young men and women who identify themselves as "science fiction freaks," sat enthralled as she expounded her ideas on "World Making."

"The idea of world-making makes me think of making a new world, a different world, something like middle-earth or the planets of science fiction—that is the work of the fantastic imagination. Or you can turn it around and say, what about making the world new, making the world different? That is the mark of the political imagination. Then you've got utopia, dystopia or whatever. But what about making the not-new? What about making this world, this old world that we live in? The old world is made new at the birth of every baby and is made new every New Year's Day. In a day-to-day living sense, we make the world we inhabit. But I have to leave it to the philosophers to decide whether we make it from scratch. It tastes like a scratch world. That's Bishop Berkeley's cosmic mix.

"What artists do is make a skillful selection of fragments of the cosmos, unusually useful and entertaining fragments of the cosmos, arranged to give an illusion of coherence and permanence. An artist makes the world, her world; an artist makes her world *the* world for a little while. Like a crystal, a work of art seems to contain everything and to imply eternity, but I think it's a fake. It's an explorer's sketch book; it's a chart of the shorelines on a foggy coast. To make something is to invent or discover it. Michaelangelo cuts away the extra marble that hides the statue, right? Now I tried reversing this, which I think we do less often. To discover something is to invent it. Julius Caesar said, 'The existence of Britain was uncertain until I went there.' We can safely agree that the ancient Britons probably were fairly certain that Britain was there. But it does depend upon how you look at it, and as far as Rome was concerned, Caesar *did* invent Britain. He made it because he got there.

"Think of Alexander the Great...I don't suppose anybody here is old enough to have read *Fifty Famous Stories*. I don't know who wrote it. It's a little tiny book you read when you're about six, and my entire knowledge of world history comes from it. And now I will tell you a story that comes from *Fifty Famous Stories*. Alexander the Great sat down and cried (and as far as I can figure, he was somewhere in the middle of India) because there were no new worlds to conquer. What a stupid, silly man! There he was, sitting and sniffling half way to China, and then he turned back. Alexander the Great was a conqueror. Conquerors are always running into new worlds and then they are running out of them. Conquest is not finding and conquest is not making. Our culture, which conquered what is called the New World and which sees the natural world, the world nature, as an adversary to be conquered, look at us now! We are running out of everything. I have been thinking about 'Lost Worlds and Future Worlds' and realize that I can't get to the future worlds without the lost worlds. We are the children of the conquerors. We live here in the Americas; we are the inhabitants of a lost world. It's totally lost, even the names are lost. The people who lived here on these hills where we are now—10,000 or 20,000 or 30,000 or 40,000 years ago—we haven't got the carbon dating down yet—how are they remembered? They are remembered in the language of the conquistadores. They are the Santa Claras, the San Franciscos; they are remembered by the names of foreign demigods. Sixty-three years ago my father wrote that the Cossano Indians are extinct so far as all practical purposes are concerned. A few scattered individuals survive. This period of sixty-three years has sufficed to efface even traditional recollections of the forefathers' habits except for occasional fragments. Here is one such fragment preserved in my father's book. It was a song which they sang somewhere around the San Francisco bay under the live oaks. Originally there weren't any wild oaks here, these oaks are European. There were different weeds on the hill. 'I dream of you, I dream of you jumping rabbit, jack rabbit, and quail....' Then in the same chapter on the Cossano Indians, there is one line from a dancing song. 'Dancing on the brink of the world.' When I was a kid and when I was a young writer, I knew I had to have a past to make a future with, and I didn't know where to go for it. I went to the European culture of my own forefathers and my own mothers. I took what I could from them and I learned as I went on to filch, to steal, to grab anything I could—from China, from Japan, from India, the idea of the wave from China, the dancing god from India, anything I could use to patch together a world. But what I'd like to say now is that there is still a mystery in the place where you are born, the place where you grow up, and Berkeley is where I was born and grew up. My world, my California, it still isn't me. To make a new world you've got to start with an old one. I don't think there is any question about that. To find a world, maybe you have to get lost. The dance they danced in California, the dance of renewal, the dance that renewed the world every spring was always danced on the brink, on the edge, on the foggy coast.

"California has influenced me totally and utterly! I went East to college and I think in some ways I felt more alien in the Northeast than I did even in France where I went after college for graduate work. I had planned to be a college teacher of French and Italian language and literature. I don't want chauvinism to creep up on me from behind, but I feel very Western. You'd think growing up in Manhattan would force you to utopia. I love New York City, that's a good city. It's next best to London. But living there is hard. It's just so much easier to get along on the West Coast."

"When I talk about my parents, I always feel like I'm boasting. I happened to be born, luckily enough, to my father, Alfred Kroeber, who was an anthropologist. He grew up in Manhattan and got his doctorate under Franz Boas at Columbia and happened to get a job in California, which was way-out at that time, about 1904 or 1906, and he lived the rest of his life out here, first writing at the museum in San Francisco and always affiliated with U.C. Berkeley. He did his ethnology mostly among the Indians of California and his archeology in Peru. He had an early marriage and his first wife died very young of tuberculosis before the First World War. Then getting on to fifty, he took a second wife who was Theodora, my mother. She had had two children of her own earlier and then she had two children with him; so I have two older half-brothers and a brother. There were four kids in the family and when they got us all raised and married and sent off, then my mother, Theodora, started writing and wrote a best seller, somewhat to her own surprise and immensely to the surprise of the U.C. Press which published *Ishi, In Two Worlds* and didn't know what to do when it appeared on the *New York Times* best seller list. I think they were sort of humiliated."

Although Theodora was not an anthropologist by training, she had taken a course in anthropology with Professor Kroeber as a part of her work for a Masters in Social Psychology. That classroom encounter led to the marriage and produced the family whose shared interest in cultures was to exert a profound influence on Ursula LeGuin's life and writing.

"I grew up amongst anthropologists, Indians, refugees from Nazi Germany, crazy ethnologists. The best family friend was an Indian who came to stay with us for six weeks every summer. He was just a member of the family. I actually thought I was related to Juan. You know how kids are, they take all of this for granted. Obviously, something seeped through, a kind of cultural relativism, a kind of nobody really has the word but everybody's word is worth listening to. And then I think something genetic also happened because I don't know about my mother—my mother is so sneaky, I can't put my finger on her at all. She is beyond me, entirely. As for my father, I physically resembled him and I'm interested in artifacts, just as he was. He liked to know how a thing was made, what it was made for, why it was made that way. This comes into my fiction all of the time. It's where my fiction often starts from, small artifacts. I know I inherited this, but my father did it with real things while I make them up.

"I guess I had a fortunate upbringing, an incredibly lucky childhood. I've been told that Tillie Olsen recently talked here about luck in a writer's life, and that touched me very much because, God knows, I was lucky. If I can draw on the springs of 'magic,' it's because I grew up in a good place, in a good time even though it was the Depression, with parents and siblings who didn't put me down, who encouraged me to drink from the springs. I was encouraged by my father, by my mother. I was encouraged to be a woman, to be a writer, to be any damn thing I wanted. Even by my brothers, although they sometimes did put me down because they were older, but only to a certain extent.

"My writing started when my next oldest brother taught me how to write. I think I more or less started when I learned the alphabet, at five. You wouldn't believe how awful it was. I started sending things out for publication at about 18. I got some poetry published in little poetry magazines. That was partly because my father kept kicking me and saying 'come on, come on, you can't keep putting everything in the attic. If you're a writer, you're a writer. People have to read what you write.' He really goaded me and in fact acted as my agent for a couple of years.

"It's a lot of work sending writing out, it's a *lot* of work! You have to keep a record of whom you're sending to, what you've sent, and when it comes back, what they said, and then whom you send it to next. He was a methodical person and he rather enjoyed this and he taught me how to do it; until I got a literary agent I used his system. Anyway, when I was in my early twenties, I got a little poetry published. I sent things out for about ten years before I got anything published that I got paid for. Then they discovered I was a science fiction writer. What do you know! I was in like Flynn. I had a label and I could get published.

"By that time I was getting pretty hungry for a market. You get on towards thirty and you've written all these years and you haven't published anything except bits and pieces and one short story in an academic journal. There comes a point when you either publish or you stop, and I was getting near that point. Then I realized that science fiction was different from when I had stopped reading it at twelve. There were some very neat new writers and new science fiction magazines, and I said, 'maybe these magazines would take my stuff.' And sure enough they did—so I came in as a science fiction writer and God bless science fiction because I probably never would have gotten published. They wouldn't have known what to call me because I wrote such weird stuff, and publishers and book sellers need labels. They have to know what section to put it in in the bookstore. That's a fact of life.

"By now I have written science fiction, hard science fiction, soft science fiction, juvenile fiction, truly juvenile. I've got a kid's picture book out. I've got young adult fiction. When I was reviewing Doris Lessing's last two books from the Shikasta series, I found that she has discovered what I, to my great joy, had discovered a little earlier: that (a) if you're writing what they call science fiction, you're absolutely free—you can write anything you damn please, and (b) that if you take seriously the science fiction premise, you are furnished with an inexhaustable supply of absolutely beautiful and complex metaphors for our present situation, for who and where we are now, and I think it's not only women who have found this out. Angus Wilson was one of the first to do this with *The Old Man in the Zoo* years ago. That is a science fiction novel, if you look at it closely. Several of the writers who interest me most are doing this sort of thing, but Lessing has done it wholeheartedly and courageously. I love her introduction that says academics put science fiction down and to hell with them! That's really nice coming from Doris Lessing.

"I'm getting awfully choosy in my science fiction reading at this point; I have read too much. It's not science fiction's fault, it's my fault. I've O.D.'d on it. I'm full up. I know all the plots. But there are some writers I can read without question and with pleasure and joy, like Vonda McIntyre. Or Jean Wolf. The current Jean Wolf in print is a collection of short stories called *The Island of Dr. Death and Other Stories*. I think Jean is one of the major novelists of the eighties. She's working on a trilogy which is going to be called *The Book of the New Sun*. I think we have something inexhaustible being written under our very eyes. And, with a kind of bitterness in my heart, I have to say that I think probably the best American science fiction writer alive is still Phillip K. Dick, although he let me down really badly when he turned against abortion rights and women. He still is a superb artist, one of the best novelists we have got. My favorite is *The Martian Time Slip*. This is a man who has never been recognized by any critic of any stature. He has never had a decent edition of any of his books. They come out in these ratty little paper backs with gaudy covers and go out of print again, but I tell you, he is one of the best we've got going.

"I think the critics are lagging. There's an awful lot of schlocky science fiction, God knows, baloney ground out from the baloney factory. Let's have another sword and sorcery book, which is about the level the movies have just reached. But the critics are lagging in that they have ignored Phillip K. Dick and McIntyre and Wolf. They're just not looking at the stuff. They're taking the easy way out and saying 'that's science fiction, I won't read it.' That's stupid. You should never dismiss any book because it happens to have been published with a certain label on it. My God, you could publish *Wuthering Heights* among the gothic romances. It *is* a gothic romance. You could reissue it and would the critics pay any attention? No."

LeGuin was asked to say something about how feminists might proceed in the creating of new worlds.

"Since Tuesday, election day, when Ronald Reagan was elected, I'm wearing my ERA button everywhere. We have got to come awake again. We've got to work really hard. That's all I know, but in what exact ways, I don't know."

Mellor commented that we could do worse than follow what LeGuin called Odonanism in *The Dispossessed* and wondered whether LeGuin still felt the society founded on Anarres is a viable utopian vision for us.

"Odonanism is roughly identifiable with anarchism. I think it is a fairly identifiable form of the anarchist lineage of Kropotkin, Emma Goldmann and, to a large extent, Paul Goodman. It's passivist anarchism, an identifiable tradition, not Bakhunism. It's just that nobody else had ever used it for fiction — it seemed such a pity. Well, the problem of anarchism, as the Marxists have consistently pointed out, is how do you get there? It's lovely once you're there. You know, the only place it has been wisely and seriously tried is Spain, and look what happened to Spain in the 1930s. Once you ask how we can practice it, I'm afraid my realism takes over.

"I made the proponent of Odonanism a woman. Do you want to know something humiliating? In a partial first draft of the novel Odo was male, and I was consistently uncomfortable and uneasy with Odo. Then I realized: 'you're not a man at all,' and then it all just flowed like milk and honey, but I was obeying my cultural imperatives which say that people who invent things, who get large ideas and spread them, were men, and it took an act of will to get around it."

In response to a question about the relation between the sexes on Anarres, LeGuin said that it was "egalitarian." Then she exclaimed, "God, how can you do anarchism in a few sentences! Men and women are people; they meet on equal ground; approach each other on equal ground. All choices, all options are open. The point about anarchism is that you don't close any doors, and this of course demands a great deal of the people who try to live by it.

"About the couple relationship, I guess I'm fascinated by marriage in the larger sense of the word. Human beings do seem to sort themselves out into pairs as their life goes on, and yet at age 51 now, I'm very much caught between two cultural norms, one which was a pair-bonding one since I grew up in a very closely pair-bonded family and this is, to some extent, still an ideal to me. Two people who are really happy together is a lovely thing, and I guess I was interested in showing that. And because I was trying to write a utopia, a happy place, a good place, I wanted a happy couple in it."

In *The Left Hand of Darkness* LeGuin explores the possibility of biological androgyny, as opposed to an egalitarian society.

"To put it extremely crudely, it's as if human beings were cats or dogs, and we went into heat once a month, but in between heat, you're asexual or nonsexual and in heat you can go either male or female every time. One time you might sire a child and the next month you might become pregnant and nine months later bear one, and these options are open until menopause. Of course, what that means is that in the society in which those androgynes live, there are no sex-linked occupations since everybody can be male or female at any time."

Although the androgynes are biologically both male and female in *The Left Hand of Darkness*, they are invariably referred to in the masculine, by use of the generic "he." LeGuin was asked if she would now change anything in the book to cope with this linguistic problem.

"Actually, in my feedback from it, I found a strange variation on that. Most men happily accept all the Gethenians as male, but women vary about it. If I wrote it again, I would change a lot of things I couldn't do then. You can't go fiddling around with something you wrote fifteen years ago before there was a women's movement. I would play a lot more with the children. That's what I left out. I got so fascinated with my political plot that I left the kids out. Stupid. I would not change my use of pronouns. I did that, you may know, when I was given the opportunity of reprinting a short story called *Winter's King* which was a prelude to *The Left Hand of Darkness*. It was before I really noticed they were all called 'he' and when I got to reprint it, I refer to the King and others as 'she.' I called it 'King' and then I called it 'she,' and this was a lot of fun. I've had a lot of feedback from that edition, but I don't honest to goodness think it makes much difference. It's always a gamble whether my imagination works. Every novel is a collaboration between the writer and the reader, right? And I had to ask a whole lot of the readers of *The Left Hand of Darkness* to try to put themselves into the shoes of an androgynous person throughout the book. I gave men a very easy out. I had this kind of callow male earthling hero. Women, I didn't give an easy out. I thought that they, like me, would find it very easy to be androgynous and actually, to a large extent, that's true. And to a certain extent, men have identified not with Genly Ai, the male, but also with Estraven, the androgyne. It was a gamble, it still is a gamble."

Both *The Dispossessed* and *The Left Hand of Darkness* are set in extremely barren climates. Anarres is set on the moon where it is dusty and sterile and nothing grows, and in *The Left Hand of Darkness* it's always freezing. LeGuin was asked why she had placed those potentially feminist utopian societies in such harsh environments.

"I don't know. I honestly don't know. I've been asked this before. I have tried to think about it before. It's my utopia, my place where I want to be. I don't know why. All I can say is this: the South Sea islands, the place where everybody dreams of going, where the fruits drop off the trees and men and women are both available and everything is warm, comfortable, and easy, has always absolutely revolted me. Somehow, I crave the other. Maybe because I'm a Californian. I grew up in utopia. I've moved north. I moved to Portland where it snows a little, and I like it."

In most of LeGuin's novels, the major protagonists are not, in fact, female, but male. LeGuin was asked if she found herself thinking through male protagonists or whether she used them ironically.

"Again, I don't know and again it's something I've given enormous thought to because I wrote a couple of my major books before the woman's movement was going. When it came up in the late sixties and through the seventies, it forced me to question everything I had taken for granted, everything about myself, everything about my writing. And I have not come out with very satisfactory answers. I know one reason I use males is the same reason that I use aliens in alien planets—I like to distance. There is something evasive, apparently, about me that wants to write through a distanced protagonist. When I have written books with a female protagonist, I feel totally different about the book. I feel a curious vulnerability and unsureness about the book always. In other words, I'm more vulnerable if I'm writing as a woman and there's a lot of defensiveness going on. It could be that I'm working towards being able to write as a woman, who knows? I really don't know."

Referring to another book, *The Lathe of Heaven*, in which dreams become effective, LeGuin was asked what relationship she saw between our dream life and the real world.

"It's all the same thing. There is no distinction. Western culture has tended to discount the dream, to a really psychotic extent. It's time that the dream was reoccupying its proper kingdom." LeGuin admitted that she sometimes used her own dreams in her writing. "Not like Robert Louis Stevenson, who actually called upon them and summoned them. Jeckyl and Hyde came from a dream zone. But usually when I'm writing, I don't dream very much because it's all going into the writing."

Although LeGuin tended to discount the distinction between dream-world and "real" world, she made a sharp distinction between the real world and the world of science fiction. When asked if there is really a difference between what we call reality and science fiction, she retorted decisively: "You bet you there is. You keep that firmly in mind. It's a fiction. You know what Marianne Moore said about imaginary gardens with real toads—sometimes there are real gardens with imaginary toads in them. But it's a mixture. Fiction writers write fiction, particularly in science fiction. People forget this and say they are describing reality or they are predicting reality. But the very most that a fiction writer can do is offer an option."

URSULA LEGUIN, 1929–

Selected Bibiography
Fiction and Science Fiction
PLANET OF EXILE. New York: Ace Double, 1966.
ROCANNON'S WORLD. New York: Ace Double, 1966.
CITY OF ILLUSIONS. New York: Ace, 1967.
A WIZARD OF EARTHSEA. Berkeley: Parnassus Press, 1968.
THE LEFT HAND OF DARKNESS. New York: Ace, 1969.
THE LATHE OF HEAVEN. New York: Charles Scribner's Sons, 1971.
THE TOMBS OF ATUAN. New York: Atheneum, 1971.
THE FARTHEST SHORE. New York: Atheneum, 1972.
FROM ELFLAND TO POUGHKEEPSIE. Portland: Pendragon Press, 1973.
THE DISPOSSESSED: AN AMBIGUOUS UTOPIA. New York: Harper
    and Row, 1974.
LEESE WEBSTER. New York: Atheneum, 1979.
THE BEGINNING PLACE. New York: Bantam, 1981.
Short Stories
THE WIND'S TWELVE QUARTERS. New York: Harper and Row, 1975.
Poetry
WILD ANGELS. Santa Barbara: Capra Press, 1975.
HARD WORDS AND OTHER POEMS. New York: Harper and Row,
    1981.

Jessamyn West

FROM A PUBLIC DIALOGUE BETWEEN WEST
AND JENNIFER CHAPMAN, STANFORD UNDERGRADUATE,
NOVEMBER 12, 1980.

Jessamyn West published her first book at the age of forty-three. She has since written more than eighteen. They include novels, short stories, poetry, science fiction, memoirs, screen plays, and one opera libretto. Her most recent book, *Double Discovery*, is an auto-biographical account of her experiences during the summer of 1929 when she attended a literary workshop at Oxford University.

Jessamyn was born in 1902 in Indiana, the first child of Eldo Roy and Grace Anna Milhous West. From her mother's family Jessamyn inherited a Quaker lineage and a family relationship to President Richard Milhous Nixon. Her father taught school in Indiana and, after moving to California in 1909, achieved a certain measure of prosperity through various enterprises, including citrus farming and real estate. Jessamyn grew up in Southern California, attended Fullerton High School, and graduated from Whittier College. Later she worked toward a Ph.D in English literature at the University of California at Berkeley.

In 1923 she married Harry Maxwell McPherson, also from a Quaker background. Together they have lived for more than half a century in the California coastal area, he as an educator and she as a writer. In Napa, where he was for many years the Superintendent of Schools, she is known as Mrs. McPherson. Elsewhere he is known as Dr. West.

Chapman read a statement West had made about the task of speech-making when she had given a lecture at Stanford twenty-five years earlier.

"Why do I do it? Because it is difficult. Because unconsciously I remember something, remember that once in a while, midway in a speech, something strange happens . . . one more speech or so and I should be wise."

West's immediate retort to this introduction was character-istically testy: "I'm not dead sure what I am supposed to comment on. Am I supposed to comment on language and its importance to me? Of course, for anyone who reads or who writes, the whole of it begins with language, begins with a word. You cannot write without using words. You use words to put landscape on paper, to put people on paper, to have them talk. As a reader that is all you have. You open the page, and see a line of words. It is in the words that we remember the great writers. We remember them not only because of the episodes and happenings in their books, but because somehow they had a great facility for putting together the words that convey to you exactly what that particular human being, or that particular summer afternoon, or that particular child's birth, meant to someone."

Chapman asked how West was able to combine a very active life as a speaker and teacher with a love of solitude and a need to write.

"You don't know how you appreciate solitude after you have been speaking or teaching all day. You need it, you require it. I suppose different people have different responses to solitude. The desire to be alone must have always been present in me. There is a piece of me that would like to be a stand-up comedian, and that part and the one who loves solitude get in the way of each other. If there is no one to whom I can be a stand-up comedian, then at least I can be alone. I remember when my father and mother in 1908 first came to California from the backwoods of Southern Indiana—it was the first automobile for them as it was for a lot of people—and California was a new place for them to explore. About four-fifths of the time I didn't want to go with them. I wanted to be alone. In one of my books I wrote of how I made for myself a place of solitude in the piano box; it was the box in which the piano that my mother was very proud of had arrived. That was my little house that I could live in. Somebody asked me recently, 'Did you mother keep the piano box in the house?,' which of course she didn't. The piano box was about as big as the house. It was outside and I could get into the piano box and see out. It was private and was my own."

Like Janet Lewis and Tillie Olsen, who as young adults also had bouts of tuberculosis, West revealed that the experience of prolonged illness had a profound influence on her writing and her life. "Well, I don't know whether or not, except for that experience, I would ever have written. I wanted to write from the time I was ten years old, but I never told anyone. I had never seen a living writer. I had never seen anyone who *had* seen a living writer, and I thought that for me to dream of writing, of putting pen to paper and from those words to have human beings come into existence, that was too vain, too pretentious. I could never do that. I never talked to my family about it, but when I graduated from college, I went to the University of California to work for my doctorate because I knew there were people who loved books there. There were libraries with stacks of books. The time came for my Ph.D. oral exam, but it had to be postponed because somebody on the committee was ill. Meanwhile, I had a large hemorrhage which was diagnosed as far-advanced T.B. and within three days I was in a sanitarium. Now, whether or not I would have ever had the backbone or the guts or whatever it takes to stick your neck out and take a chance and maybe make a fool of yourself without that having happened, I don't know. At that time, with far-advanced tuberculosis, they put you in the terminal ward. I thought my life was over. Instead, for me, it was the beginning of my life.

"I was ill, too ill even to read, let alone write, for quite a long time. But I did begin to get better and one day a woman said to me, 'Jessamyn, don't you think it would be a nice thing for you to piece a quilt so that you could leave something for your mother to remember you by?' So I thought that if things had advanced to this stage, I would pick up my pen instead of my needle, and I did just that. So you see, I really do not know what my life would have been like if I had not had this kick from the rear of a disease that made it impossible for me to do anything else except piece quilts or write.

"First of all, just in the matter of dying, which is important, you don't do much. They sent me home, it's true. They needed beds in those days. That was before they had discovered any medicine to give you for tuberculosis. I was married, but my husband couldn't give up his work to be a nurse, and my mother did not intend to have one of her loved ones die, and I was afraid to die around her. Really. She lied to me. She'd look at the thermometer and tell me each day that my temperature was getting better and better. She would put an egg in the orange juice so that in addition to drinking orange juice, I was eating an egg. She told me I didn't have to live in a sick room.

"My mother was born in Indiana and she was homesick for the East. While I was sick I lived that East of her past which seemed so romantic to me. For the most part, people think that California is the romantic land. You come here where there are oranges and palm trees, where there used to be camels down in Palm Desert. But, anyway, my mother talked about Southern Indiana, where they didn't have ground squirrels and barley stubble and trap door spiders, but where it snowed and they had bushy-tailed squirrels running around in trees. If she had not had four children, poor health, and a lot of other things, she would have made a far better writer than I. Whatever good writing takes, she had it. So I listened to her stories, but I never told her I wanted to write. At least she saw to it that I didn't die amongst my loved ones."

When asked if she had had any difficulty getting her first book published, West responded: "I was the luckiest woman in the world. I had no difficulty. First of all, I didn't have a book. I wrote short stories. Martha Foley, who edited *Best Short Stories* in the old days, had in the back of her books a list of the ten magazines that had published the most distinguished stories in the past year, and I thought, 'Oh, dear me, I wouldn't send anything to the ones at the top of the list,' but down in seventh place was a magazine called *Hairenik Weekly*. It was published in Boston, and I thought, 'here is a little magazine I have never heard of, unknown, interested in good writing. Here I am a writer, unknown, interested in good writing. We should get together.' So I sent a story to them. Immediately, back came a letter saying, 'We are entranced with your story. We think it is fine. We want to publish it; however, we are an Armenian magazine publishing the stories of young Armenians. Are you, by any chance, a young Armenian using a pseudonym?' Well, by this time I wasn't even young, but Napa is a long way from Boston, and I thought, 'The door has opened a crack to a literary career. Am I not going to have enough nerve to walk through that crack?' George Eliot, you know, she was not a man. Joseph Conrad was not an Englishman; he was a Pole with a name *that* long. They had enough nerve. So I looked through the phone book of Napa, hunting Armenian names which I could use. It's full of good Italian people making wine, but no Armenian names. If they had wanted an Italian writer, I would now be the author of *The Godfather*, but they didn't. So finally I told them the bitter truth; I am not an Armenian. And that very nice editor, for a number of years after that, whenever he saw a story of mine in some magazine, would write me and say 'I just want to congratulate you. You're doing very well, in spite of the fact that you're not an Armenian.'"

This led to the discussion of her Quaker background, highly evident in her first book, *The Friendly Persuasion*. "There were a lot of people who liked it. Then they were horribly disappointed because they thought the second book they would read would be another good, sweet, wholesome, friendly persuasion, and it didn't turn out that way. So they were disappointed. Then there were people who didn't like anything about sad, gray, unlaughing, 'theeing' and 'thying' Quakers in the first place, and once they had had one look at a book like *The Friendly Persuasion*, they didn't ever want to see another one. So, in a sense, I fell between two stools as far as readers go, and I would rather have had them face the fact that I write various things. Sometimes they're Quakers, sometimes they aren't. That would have been easier for me.

"I edited for Viking an anthology of Quaker writings. I was amazed to discover there were no Quaker novels. Young Quakers were urged to stay away from that sort of thing—there are plenty of serious things to read without mulling around in fiction. It is very hard for me to know about the Quaker influence. Probably it would be easier for someone else who has read what I have written. I never look inside a book once it's written, and I even forget them.

"I'll tell you a funny story. Some of you probably have heard Robert Cromley, who has a television program from Chicago and who reviews and interviews writers. Once about a year and a half after *Massacre at Fall Creek* had been written, he interviewed me in Chicago. He had read the book, I think, the night before. Meanwhile, I had forgotten everything. I didn't know the characters' names, I didn't know the battles, I didn't know who was an Indian and who was a white. He was very kind and very polite and helped me through, reminding me of what happened where. At the end of the program, I'm quite sure everybody thought Cromley wrote that book.

"Evidently I wasn't a good enough Quaker. I should have had the nerve and the backbone, if I wanted to write, to start writing, because women Quakers in the past did things that women even today are thought better of to let alone. They could preach from the beginning. Today we are still discussing whether a woman should preach or not. A Quaker woman could preach. No one thought anything of it. Quaker women went to jails, where no one before had gone, to read the Bible to men who were locked up, and people were extremely shocked. They thought that male offenders shut away from women for decades—that the sight of these women would rouse them to a high pitch of lust, but they didn't know Quaker women. Nothing happened. Except that some of the prisoners did do some Bible reading they hadn't done before. And women could go on missionary tours with men who weren't their husbands, and this was thought all right. I'll tell you one illustrative story. I read in the library of the Friends Meeting House in London a letter which had been written by a person, possibly from Wales, who had been the host or hostess of my great-great-grandmother, who was a Quaker minister. She was in Wales and Ireland and England, preaching, and this letter said: 'You should see her husband Amos, when she comes home tired and weary from a day or evening of preaching, he has her chair ready by the fire and her comfortable slippers already out.' It sounded very much like the reversal of roles that we are becoming accustomed to now."

When asked if she considered herself a feminist, West answered: "If I saw you getting only seventy-five cents an hour for something that a man was getting a dollar for, I would be an immediate feminist. But in a different way, I feel that I have personally accomplished a lot of things that other people still haven't yet grasped, and I can make real hardworking honest-to-goodness feminists mad because I know that this doesn't exist for everyone, and that simply because I feel free doesn't mean that I shouldn't be out in a line walking with people, trying to attain for them what I take for granted."

Chapman said, "But you've written that, being a woman, you sometimes feel a certain amount of guilt that gets in the way of your writing. For instance, you wrote, 'I wish I could unlearn the need to straighten the house before writing.' That seems to contradict what you're saying."

West countered: "Where is anything contradictory about wanting to sit down in the midst of something that is pleasing to the eye? Answer that, please!"

Chapman asked, "What about the fact that you didn't tell anyone you wanted to write until you were 26? You said you thought you were somewhat mad initially for having an urge to write, and I wonder if those feelings of responsibility for the house and the fear of admitting you wanted to be a writer are both tied to your being a woman."

West replied, "I don't tie them to either one. I had a sister, and I think a writer would be lucky if she could be born this way, who didn't give a damn if things are in a wild clutter. She wouldn't have been bothered if there were a pair of shoes on the mantel, but as it happens, I am not that way. I wouldn't feel happy writing until I took the shoes off the mantel and put them down where I thought they belonged. That is just a piece of my temperament. I don't understand the house not being orderly, because that's like painting a picture. It's making something beautiful. That is what I feel about straightening a house."

Referring to her most recent book, *Double Discovery*, which recounts her trip to England in 1929 when she had already been married for several years, West said, "I decided to strike out on my own because my husband wouldn't go with me and I didn't know anybody else who had enough money to go. I went because I had always wanted to write, though I couldn't tell anybody about it. I don't know why. It seemed pretentious, almost sacrilegious. And in the colleges I went to, there were no courses in American literature. There was one professor who thought O. Henry was pretty good! But there were plenty of courses in English literature, where one read Hardy and the Brontë sisters. So I wanted, for that reason, to go to England where the writers lived. The other reason I wanted to go there was that Oxford University had a summer session.

"It was difficult to get in. I've talked to people since then who've asked 'how did you get in?' I don't know how I got in. I was lucky. I got in anyway. And while I was gone, my husband thought he would do something useful, like go to the University at Berkeley and get his doctorate. Which he did. Of course, not in one summer. I was already writing then, that summer of '29. I wrote in my journal, and I wrote numerous letters, which my mother saved, but she didn't tell me. When she died, there was a big package and on the outside was written 'Jessamyn's letters, precious, save.' So they were then given to me, and one winter in Hawaii for three or four weeks with my husband I took those along, and I discovered letters which seemed to me from another woman. This was a young woman who hadn't previously traveled, and who was discovering Europe and Oxford for the first time, and I was now an older woman, a much older woman, discovering the young woman. That's why the book is called *Double Discovery*. It was a young woman's discovery of travel in Europe and the older woman's discovery of the young woman."

Autobiographical works constitute an important portion of West's writing. In addition to *Double Discovery* she had written the moving account of her own experience of tuberculosis and of her sister's death from cancer in the book *The Woman Said Yes*. She spoke of the genesis of that work at a time when it was less common to write first person accounts of illness and death, and explained how the book got its title. "At first I gave it another title, because my sister had written me a letter that began: 'Sister, Dear Sister, come home and help me die.' And that was what I was going to call it, or at least the 'Sister, Dear Sister' part. But the publishers did not think anybody was going to want to buy a book with a title like that, and I did not want to write a book that no one would want to buy. So between us I gave up the original title and they suggested the other title, and it also allowed me to bring my mother into the picture, which the first one hadn't been able to do as well."

Despite the fact that she has written memoirs, short stories, science fiction and poetry, West prefers the medium of the novel. "I chose the novel because my first book which was published before *The Friendly Persuasion* was a collection of short stories, and the publisher said, 'If we publish the short stories, will you deliver a novel to us?' Well, I didn't know how to write a novel, but I said 'yes' and then I had to write a novel. And really, novel writing is easier than short story writing. More can be put into the novel. When you think of the novels you have read and the short stories you have read, if you want to list the ones that really stayed with you, a novel would certainly be at the top of the list rather than some short story."

As she considered the literary figures who had influenced her writing, the names of Thoreau and Virginia Woolf were most prominent. "There are some writers whose words seem to be sculptured exactly to go twirling around in your own private understanding ear and, for me, Thoreau was one. What he had to say was as if he had whispered it just to me. Of course, it was not only the way he used language, it was the things he wrote about and the things that he loved. He too was a man who loved solitude, and as much as he wrote about travel, he didn't travel. He stayed at home. Even when he lived at Walden, he just lived down the road. Virginia Woolf was a genius in the use of words. I probably never read her with as much attention and dedication as I did Thoreau, but these were both writers I could lay my hands on at a time when I wanted books a great deal."

Comparing Thoreau's sense of nature to her own, West spoke of herself as a person who has a strong sense of Western identity, "not West Coast, just West." Although originally from Indiana, she has spent most of her life in the West and feels that her sensibility has been marked by the openness of the Western landscape.

"I was born back East. This is what Western people call the Mid-West. Somebody said, maybe I wrote it myself...I hope I did...that he could not tolerate a land where earth and sky did not meet; I found back East places where earth and sky never had a chance to meet. It was just trees, trees, trees. I don't know why somebody didn't get out and cut down a few. What could I see out of the window unless the wind blew a leaf off? I couldn't see anything that weren't leaves. Once I stayed for a short time in New England, and then I went down to Kentucky, and there began the Mid-West. There earth and sky touched and there I realized that I truly was a Westerner. I want space. I want light. I like sea, but I also like mesa and the desert. I like openness. I like mountains, not bang up against me, the way some of them are in New England, but on the horizon. So I feel like a Westerner, not necessarily West Coast, but also Montana, the John Day Country in Oregon, those long stretches of land where there is room for all of us who have crowded in here. I don't know whether that is because as a young person I lived in Southern California, which was still barley stubble land with no water—my father carried water in a barrel—it was the only water we had in the house. This feeling about wanting openness is probably the result of having lived in the West when I was young."

West said that she came to writing with an unspoken desire to give expression to many deeply felt, barely conscious sensations, and that ultimately, like most writers, she wanted to write about herself. "I suppose I wanted to write about a million things. I wanted to say, for instance, how the wind sounded. I've always thought the wind was beautiful. I wanted to write like Thoreau if I could. Write about ants fighting. I wanted to write about love, but I didn't, and it's a damn good thing I didn't try because I didn't know how to do it at all. But I'm sure that every writer wants, in a way, to reveal himself."

JESSAMYN WEST, 1902–

Selected Bibliography

Fiction

THE FRIENDLY PERSUASION. New York: Harcourt, Brace and Company, 1945.

THE WITCH DIGGERS. New York: Harcourt, Brace and Company, 1951.

THE READING PUBLIC. New York: Harcourt, Brace and Company, 1952.

CRESS DELAHANTY. New York: Harcourt, Brace and World, 1953.

LOVE, DEATH AND THE LADIES' DRILL TEAM. New York: Harcourt, Brace and World, 1955.

TO SEE THE DREAM. New York: Harcourt, Brace and World, 1957.

LOVE IS NOT WHAT YOU THINK. New York: Harcourt, Brace and World, 1959.

SOUTH OF THE ANGELS. New York: Harcourt, Brace and World, 1960.

A MATTER OF TIME. New York: Harcourt, Brace and World, 1966.

THE CHILEKINGS. New York: Ballantine Books, 1967.

LEAFY RIVERS. New York: Harcourt, Brace and World, 1967.

EXCEPT FOR ME AND THEE. New York: Harcourt, Brace and World, 1967.

CRIMSON RAMBLERS OF THE WORLD, FAREWELL. New York: Harcourt, Brace, Jovanovich, 1970.

Memoirs

HIDE AND SEEK: A CONTINUING JOURNEY. New York: Harcourt, Brace, Jovanovich, 1973.

THE WOMAN SAID YES: ENCOUNTERS WITH LIFE AND DEATH. New York: Harcourt, Brace, Jovanovich, 1976.

THE LIFE I REALLY LIVED. New York: Penguin, 1979.

DOUBLE DISCOVERY, A JOURNEY. New York: Harcourt, Brace, Jovanovich, 1980.

Poetry

THE SECRET LOOK. New York: Harcourt, Brace, Jovanovich, 1974.

Edited Work

THE QUAKER READER. New York: The Viking Press, 1962.

Libretti

A MIRROR FOR THE SKY: AN OPERA BASED ON AN ORIGINAL CONCEPTION OF RAOUL PENE DUBOIS FOR PORTRAYING THE LIFE OF AUDUBON IN A MUSICAL DRAMA. New York: Harcourt, Brace and Company, 1948.

Works About the Author

David Dempsey. "Talk with Jessamyn West." NEW YORK TIMES BOOK REVIEW, January 3, 1954.

Lee Graham. "An Interview with Jessamyn West." WRITER'S DIGEST, XLVII (May 1967), 24–27.

Brenda King. "Jessamyn West," SATURDAY REVIEW, XL(September 21, 1957), 14.

Alfred Shivers. JESSAMYN WEST. New York: Twayne Pub., Inc., 1972.

Judy Grahn

FROM A PUBLIC DIALOGUE BETWEEN GRAHN
AND JOHN FELSTINER, PROFESSOR OF ENGLISH,
STANFORD UNIVERSITY, NOVEMBER 19, 1980.

Judy Grahn is the quintessential feminist writer. The content of her poetry and her personal style were formed within the context of the women's movement in the Bay area. In the seventies she was published by several small presses and also became the publisher of other women poets, and was a frequent participant in those poetry readings which constituted public rituals for feminists, as they had for the beat writers of an earlier decade. Grahn is an inspired reader of her own work, as the reading of "Vera, From My Childhood" demonstrated.

Solemnly swearing, to swear as an oath to you
who have somehow gotten to be a pale old woman;
swearing, as if an oath could be wrapped around
your shoulders
like a new coat:
For your 28 dollars a week and the bastard boss
you never let yourself hate;
and the work, all the work you did at home
where you never got paid;
For your mouth that got thinner and thinner
until it disappeared as if you had choked on it,
watching the hard liquor break your fine husband down
into a dead joke.
For the strange mole, like a third eye
right in the middle of your forehead;
for your religion which insisted that people
are beautiful golden birds and must be preserved;
for your persistent nerve
and plain white talk—

the common woman is as common
as good bread
as common as when you couldnt go on
but did.
For all the world we didnt know we held in common
all along
the common woman is as common as the best of bread
and will rise
and will become strong—I swear it to you
I swear it to you on my own head
I swear it to you on my common
woman's
head

"'Vera, from my childhood' is one of seven poems in my
Common Woman series. I wrote them in 1969, when I had just
joined a women's consciousness-raising group. Those groups came
along at the end of the sixties and I suddenly wanted something to
read about women, but I couldn't find anything. The closest I came
was a Leonard Cohen song sung by Nina Simone—very wistful. I put
it on the record player and played it over and over and wrote those
seven poems to ordinary women I had known. I picked the word
'common' poetically because it means so many different things, and
they all come back to feminist ideals in some way. 'Common'
reminded me of 'common whore,' 'common slut' or something that's
sexual property, and 'common' also reminded me of the commons of
England and of Boston where people could meet together and assert
themselves. It reminded me of what we have in common, which is a
cross-connection between us all. And in one of the poems, I even
managed to use it as a nail, which, if you are a carpenter, you know
is called a common nail. The multiplicity of meanings gave the
poems an extra emphasis which was both poetic and real and
political, all at the same time.

Felstiner noted that the word "'common' has what so many
words suggest which political and ethnic groups have picked for
themselves lately: a hard, angry, negative thrust with a bad conno-
tation that turns itself around and says this is something we have to
stand by and be proud of."

He turned to a question that must have been in the mind of
everyone who knew Grahn's poetry: How is a man supposed to feel
when he hears a poem addressed by a woman to another woman,
especially by an openly lesbian woman?

Grahn replied, "Well, women identify with men writing about

men. There are men who write about nothing but men, and I am able to identify with them as a sister and as a daughter. I think that when men get into my poetry, which is woman-oriented, they do it in a parental sense, in a brotherly sense, and I don't think they have that much trouble." She explained that the poem to Vera was inspired by her mother, "an older woman in my past, my present and my future."

"I was born in Chicago, but I grew up in a little town in New Mexico and I was an eccentric child. I was a combination of a tomboy and a poet. I was always known as a poet. I began writing long poems that my girl scout troop acted out when I was ten or eleven. Since we were very much lacking in any extra money, I saved up my allowance to buy two items that I desperately wanted. One of them was a softball glove, but since I had no instruction, I accidentally bought a catcher's mitt. I did not want to be a catcher. I wanted to play first base, but forever after I had to be a catcher because I accidentally spent my money on a catcher's mitt. That's a really tragic story, you know. But the second item that I bought was instruction on how to write poetry. I don't even remember who wrote those books but I had all of them that I could get, and I went home and studied my craft even as a child. I hid it from the other kids. They thought it was okay that I wanted to play softball but that I wanted to be a poet was really bizarre."

When asked if she, like many male poets, had the experience of "bumming around" in her early years that influenced her later poetry, Grahn replied, "I think my position as a female and as a woman of no means whatsoever and little secretarial skills, plus being a lesbian and being militant about it—wanting to have a bill of rights that would guarantee us a place in the modern state—gave me more than bumming around; I was kicked around, I was floated around from place to place, hunting and searching, not for experience, but for a place to stop having so much experience and be able to express something. I think that for many women this is true. What took me a while was to know that my life had been a set of experiences that were worth writing about and that actually had a richness to it and connection to other people. So it wasn't bumming around that I needed but the other, the opposite, the stable society in which to say 'everything I have experienced is true,' to say it out loud so that it is confirmed as something that really matters. I needed to express what it's like to be a secretary, to make sandwiches, to want to be a scientist, and have breasts as well. How do you express all that? I think that's what women writers have been dealing with.

"Once I grew up, I wanted to go to school, but I couldn't afford it, so I became a sandwich maker and worked nights so that I could go to trade school in the daytime and become a medical secretary. Then I was a medical secretary in the daytime and I went to school at night, which is not atypical of the way that women go to school, and after a long time of doing that, I suddenly became very ill and got brain fever and went into a coma, and when I came out of my coma, I couldn't remember anything, but I was very happy, extremely happy. I remember waking up singing a little ditty from Archibald MacLeish's play, *J.B.*, that was about survivors of nuclear warfare. It had this little childish song in it: 'I love Monday, Tuesday, Wednesday, da da da...' I sang the song for a year; that was the only thing I could do, it was my only skill. And during that time I realized that if I was going to do what I had set out to do in my life, I would have to go all the way with it and take every single risk you could take. I was then twenty-five years old and I saw that I could have died a very nice ordinary woman who had produced absolutely nothing. So I bought a notebook and I got a very strange hat and I went to a local bar and told everyone I was a poet. I began taking notes and began again, and this time I decided I would not do anything I didn't want to do that would keep me from my art. And I haven't since that time. I just turned forty.

"I should probably add that I was very fortunate to have had a lover who wanted me to be a poet, and she took care of me for that year when I was in such terrible condition. She was a teacher and so we just got by. It was a very hard year. And then I did not go and become a poet until I had also gotten a part-time job as a laboratory technician.

"*Edward The Dyke* was written at that time. It was considered unpublishable, a little satire about a woman and a psychiatrist. I wrote *Edward The Dyke* in Washington, D.C. That's the white collar center of the universe. You would think that no one would ever write a lesbian feminist satire in 1965 in Washington, D.C., but I did. Since it was unpublishable, I had to wait and become a publisher myself before I could really get rolling.

"In 1969 I founded a press with Wendy Cadden, an artist, with a simple mimeograph machine. I had a little trouble learning to use it at first—it's such a classical office machine that I had avoided it for many years, not wanting to end up doing only that, but when we realized that no one was going to do our work for us, we began to design beautiful books on that mimeograph machine. We treated it as an artistic instrument, and it produced for us as an artistic instrument. We produced books of graphics and poems, deciding to find a new basis for the criticism of art and poetry.

"This was the same time I began writing *The Common Woman*

poems. I took them to my neighbors and asked them what they thought of them. I did not say that I had written them. Sometimes I just said 'Someone gave me these poems. What do you think of them?' to get female feedback. I was very courageous in those days because real people tell you real things about your work. It established a new basis for women's art—things which had formerly been unspeakable suddenly became vital and desirable things to say, and *The Common Woman* poems spread all by themselves without any help from any New York publication of any kind.

"People took them along because they wanted other people to read them. We had women who sold them on the buses, sold them at work. Women sneaked them into foreign countries because they wanted others to have them. That's what building a network of people is about—people who are just as interested in what you're doing as you are, and you help them and they help you. So much depends on making sure your work is relevant, making sure that it is useful to other people.

"*The Common Woman* poems spread: the last time I counted them was about eight years ago, and they had been reprinted half a million times from Canada to Australia and to Germany. I get letters from women in jail, women in Harvard Law School, and men in jail, men in Harvard Law School, about them and about other things. So we shifted the basis of poetry, coming out of what the beatniks had been trying to do, but they had stayed a little exclusive, and I think the women's movement and the black arts movement also shifted the basis for art and infused it with a new set of ideas and a new lifefulness. Our publishing simply magnified that. We published work of women that we thought no one else would do and we put out about sixty thousand volumes of verse on our own—isn't that amazing! Sixty thousand volumes by about 200 different women! And then we merged with another press and we kept that up for awhile. Now we've pulled away from publishing and we're concentrating on our own work."

Grahn was asked if she might still publish her own poems or have them published by another feminist press, now that she has a New York publisher, St. Martin's Press. "It keeps me very independent, which I like. It keeps me knowing that if there is an idea I really feel close to, one that is essential to what I'm doing, that I can compromise the corners of it, but I'm never going to have to compromise the center core, because I can damn well do it myself. You know, that kind of independence is pretty unbeatable. I would never have gotten anywhere if I had had to depend on New York publishers; they're very conservative to most of our ideas."

In response to a question about the West Coast publishing

scene—whether it was a good climate for women and lesbian writers—Grahn was of two minds. "Not only women and lesbian writers but many independent publishers drift out here where there has been a flourishing small press trade for many years, and flourishing poetry and flourishing political, spiritual and economic ideas. Women writing and publishing, as well as male writers and publishers, come to the West Coast and make the climate; we all hear about it and so we drift in this direction. But I think most people create their own environments. There's an environment here for publishing, but for writing? Writing takes so much determination—you would do it on a rock in the middle of the ocean, if you had to."

Remembering her first years on the West Coast, little more than a decade ago, Grahn spoke of the role she had played in the creation of feminist separatism. "I helped to found the institution of separatism for women, but it has been founded multitudes of times through the centuries. For me, it began in 1969 when we formed women-only groups and held women-only dances. We were quite daring to do that at the time. I began writing specifically about women's issues and lives, feeling that I couldn't learn to do that from men. I could only learn to do it by concentrating on women. We perceived separatism as a tool, as a home base in this very nomadic society—everyone needs one—and for women, separatism has been a home base from which to launch our various legions of issues out into society.

"I found that sometimes at women-only readings, men would dress up like women and come to my readings to hear me, which really astonished me. They would creep in in dresses. I believe this happened in antiquity and someone's mother ripped him to pieces for doing that very thing, but of course we're different now. We don't go to those extremes.

"The first time I read anything on the subject of rape where there were men in the audience, they laughed because they didn't know how else to respond. So, it was impossible to bring the subject up with men in the audience until men had learned a different set of responses and perceptions. They had to identify with rape as a problem and not want it to happen. Many people took it for granted before the women's movement that rape was okay, it was even funny; so that was one of the reasons for us to use separatism at that particular time. Now I would read a rape poem to a mixed audience on purpose because I know there would be plenty of men in the audience who identify with it, some of them who have been raped themselves, or who go out on Take-Back-The-Night marches and who are organizers on the issue."

❧

Grahn was asked if being a lesbian poet created additional problems of communication. Does she feel that she speaks for other lesbians or women in general or even some larger community?

"I don't think I speak for anyone but myself. I don't think anyone ever basically does. I mean, you have to ask someone else whether I speak for them or not, but I certainly have tried to speak about and to a large number of people, different kinds of people, whose spirits crowd into my room in their most critical aspects while I'm writing.

"Being a lesbian, which I knew I was by the time I was sixteen, and being a poet, which I knew I was when I was nine, forced me to put those two things together, and there are a number of ways to do it. I had some traumatic things happen to me as a lesbian. For example, I was thrown out of the Air Force for being honest about my lesbianism. So I felt it was very important for me to be able to find a way to speak as a lesbian and then go on from there to be everybody's poet, which is what I want to be. I had to take care of that little piece of business first. For fifteen years I've been juggling both sides of myself, trying to create a climate whereby people could see around the fact that I'm a lesbian. When this stereotype would be broken, they would understand, 'Yes, there is such a thing, and it has thus and such dimensions, and that's her or that's me, but the rest of her work is about something else which pertains to many, many other issues.' I don't know if I'm describing it, but my intention is to write poetry for everyone, and, given that, I have to do it as me. So first I have to establish that everyone can see me as who I am and take that for granted, and then we can go on to what comes next."

Commenting on the universality of Grahn's work, Felstiner read from Adrienne Rich, in her introduction to *The Work of a Common Woman*: "When I finished the poem ("A Woman Is Talking to Death") I realized I had been weeping; and I knew in an exhausted kind of way that what had happened to me was irreversible."

Her poem on Marilyn Monroe caused readers to wonder how Grahn could reconcile anger and humor. She explained: "If you have two emotions, then you know that I'm really talking about something more than just what I said I was talking about. What I'm really talking about is all of us who have seen a symbol of Hollywood success commit suicide at the height of her career, after having married an athlete and after having married an intellectual and obviously wanting to become an intellectual herself, and wanting to be someone whose body would be taken more for itself and less as the pretty horseflesh that it was taken for. When I think of her, I get a terrible chill because I know that she came from a poor background and worked her way all the way up to being a suicide, and I don't want that to happen to any of us ever again.

"I knew women similar to her, for example, a very statuesque blonde woman who was the mistress of a doctor and when he jilted her at age 40, she drank mercury and took a week to die. It was the same year as Monroe's death and that was not unusual. We should not have those kinds of images in our minds to look forward to. This poem was written to break through that poster image to another side and say, 'Let's go for what's real, let's take this and make something else out of it,' and I think that for the last decade we've been doing just that." Grahn made it clear that the anger was not directed at Marilyn Monroe but at the potential suicide "who lives in each of us."

❧

"I'm doing a lot of research into women's history and also gay history and beginning to write about that. I'm also working on a novel. It actually has many characters that are plants and animals, which I find intriguing. I seem to be really expanding the notion of how poetry can be useful to the other arts and lead us further into understanding the nature of our world: where we come from and what the basis of women's power is, what it looks like, where it developed and where it might go. At some point in the past, poets were scientists in society, and I want us to reclaim that part of poetry, the notion of being very exact in description, like druids and sorcerers and other ancient poets. They were using language in its most potent form. So I am straining, in every direction, in order to do research and combine etymology with imagery. I am trying to understand analogy, which is a way of comparing one thing to another, so that we can make connections again."

Grahn had written an article on the word "bulldyke," in conjunction with her historical research. "I don't know of an uglier word I've ever been called in my life than 'bulldyke.' I was so haunted by this for many years that I finally decided to take the word by the horns and find out why this strange word is in the vernacular. I've traced it to a Celtic queen who fought against the Romans in A.D. 61 during the reign of Nero and nearly won. The Celts had institutional gay practices, which the Roman authors were horrified by. This queen led a nation which still had gay traditions going on. She had flaming red hair and was a very large woman. The Celtic women warriors were older women who often taught the men arms. It was a totally different sense of fighting than we have any conception of. And when she rebelled against the Roman colonists and nearly won, they suppressed her name. Her name was Boadicea, a word which has come down to us meaning a very militaristic or strong, warrior-like, lesbian-type large female. That's a part of what I'm working on, combining poetry and etymology and my own experiences. There are many other examples besides that one. That's the one that really thrilled me to death when it finally came together."

Judy Grahn leaves her readers realizing, consciously or not, what people from antiquity down through the Renaissance have realized: that at her best, the poet feels no distinction between her own experience, her art, and her political life. All three feed and flow into each other.

JUDY GRAHN, 1940–

Selected Bibliography

Poetry

EDWARD THE DYKE. Oakland: Diana Press, 1971.

THE COMMON WOMAN POEMS. Oakland: Diana Press, 1974.

A WOMAN IS TALKING TO DEATH. Oakland: Diana Press, 1974.

SHE WHO. Oakland: Diana Press, 1977.

THE WORK OF A COMMON WOMAN: THE COLLECTED POETRY
     OF JUDY GRAHN, 1964–1977, with an introduction by Adrienne
     Rich. New York: St. Martin's Press, 1980.

THE QUEEN OF WANDS. Trumansburg, New York: The Crossing Press,
     1982.

Short Stories (edited)

Judy Grahn, ed. TRUE TO LIFE ADVENTURE STORIES. 3 vols. Oakland:
     Diana Press, 1978–?

Non-Fiction (edited)

Judy Grahn, ed. LESBIANS SPEAK OUT. Oakland: Diana Press, 1974.

Kay Boyle

FROM A CONVERSATION BETWEEN BOYLE
AND PHOTOGRAPHER MARGO DAVIS,
COTTAGE GROVE, OREGON, MARCH 1982.

Kay Boyle is eighty-one years old. Her life has encompassed an American girlhood early in this century, Paris in the twenties, the McCarthy era when she and her husband were both blacklisted, San Francisco in the sixties and seventies, and now Oregon. She is the mother of six children and the author of some thirty books. Boyle has taught in various institutions ranging from girls' schools to universities. During the fifties and early sixties, she taught at Miss Thomas's School in Connecticut, where Margo (Baumgarten) Davis was one of her students. Speaking with Davis some twenty years later, Boyle recalled her own experiences as a learner and teacher and expounded her personal pedagogy.

"First I taught at Miss Thomas's in Connecticut and later I spent months here and there as a writer in residence in various universities. But my pleasure in the Connecticut classes was of a special nature. There my students ranged from fourteen to eighteen years old and they permitted me as a teacher to become a part of the inexhaustible exuberance of their lives.

"Springtime is a season we tend to forget as we grow older, and yet far back in our memories, like the landscape of a country visited long ago, it's always there. It is not easy to preserve that landscape. When the girls went on to college, the change always took place. In the first year they went away, those students wrote as they did before and sent back their writing to me—poems about rebellion, essays against parents, all the things that were stirring in their minds and hearts. And then, little by little, month by month, they came, despite themselves, to recognize and accept academic patterns of thought, and they could no longer write in the same way as before.

"From the beginning, my teaching there was made easy by the advice from the founder of the school, Miss Mabel Thomas, then 90 years old, who had studied with William James. Before I took over her classes, she spoke to me about the teaching of writing. She did not use that unhappy term 'creative writing' in describing one's particular need for defining one's identity. 'There is one very simple thing that I have told my students for over 40 years,' she said. 'Perhaps you will find it useful. When you write, let it be words that would be impossible to call out when you meet one another on the school grounds or in the halls. Writing is not "hi" or "gosh" or "golly" or "it's Wednesday." It isn't even what you're doing after school. It's what you're feeling at a given moment. Writing is the recording of something that has stirred your emotions, channeled through your mind to the page so that other people may feel that emotion too. If there are students who say they do not wish to reveal their emotions to you, who resent your asking that of them, well then, respect that resentment. For this kind of consideration of the young is a part of teaching. Explain to them that an emotion can be something quite undramatic. It can be the feel of the breeze on the back of your hand when you sit by an open window in study hall. Tell them it need not be the unbearing of some dreadful despair, although it can be that, too. Tell them to walk down to the sea wall and write a page describing the feel of stones under their feet, the spray as it blows into their faces, the taste of the salt on their lips. This is what I believe writing is because it is the recounting of a lonely experience and that is where all writing begins.'

"I told Miss Thomas there was probably no one in the world less qualified than I to be a teacher. The truth is I cannot spell and I cannot parse a sentence. And I not only have no degrees, advanced or otherwise, but I never had time to go to school. Once many years ago when I wanted to take a course in English literature at Columbia University I could produce no high school certificate. I was required to attend a night class in elementary English in order to accumulate the necessary credit. My classmates in that evening course were all desperately determined to grasp the intricacies of a new tongue. Because our teacher embodied all that a teacher should not be, he has remained stirringly alive in my memory. After fifty years I can see him still in all his bigness and bitterness standing there in the classroom transmitting to us nothing but the vocabulary of his own defeat. He was given to sarcasm, perhaps the worst of all academic offenses against the eagerness and hope of the young. One evening, impatient with the class, he got up on the chair and shouted, 'the moon is made of green cheese.' Everyone including myself wrote this statement carefully down, the middle-aged, immigrant gentleman beside me spelling the last word 'chiz.' I can recall learning nothing else in that class except this undocumented piece of information about the moon and the fact that a sad man had failed as a teacher because of his failure as a human being.

"Gilbert Hyatt has written somewhere that one of the unalterable rules of teaching is that one should never undertake to teach a subject one does not know inside out. I'm not sure that I agree with him for in the course of seeking to instruct the young, I have explored philosophy, history, biology, psychology, subjects in which I have had no training. My students and I learned together many things we did not know before. In my classes we wrote poems and stories from the mind of a student of Plato. We wrote of terror from the point of view of a white wolf in the arctic, hunted by men, and from that of Marie Antoinette on her way to the guillotine. We set forth rather humbly on remarkable voyages of discovery, though I was always a little afraid to teach. And if I was always a little afraid to teach, I was saved by the fact that I was not afraid to learn.

"There are things I believe very strongly a teacher should not do. The teacher should not use a red pencil to correct a student's paper. The word correct is of course a disaster. The difference between the black of a student's writing and the red of the teacher's comment implies a difference in language and status."

Boyle's sense of the inherent equality between individuals, whether they be teacher and student or ruler and ruled, has been expressed in a life-long devotion to social justice and human rights issues. She traces her passion for social justice back to her earliest years and especially to the female influences in her life.

"I have had three tremendously interesting women in my life— my mother, my mother's sister, and their mother, my grandmother. And I just took it for granted that women took part in things. They all fought, first for the ballot for women, and then afterwards for the Equal Rights Amendment. My aunt, Nina E. Allender, who was my mother's elder sister, was the official cartoonist for the National Women's Party. Her cartoons number in the hundreds because she did them for the cover of the magazine which was first called *The Suffragist* and after that *The Equal Rights Publication*. Her cartoons are all in the Library of Congress.

"She also designed the 1936 postage stamp of Susan B. Anthony walking up the steps of the Capitol with a scroll in her hand. Anthony has a little shawl around her shoulders and a little red hat on her head. She is taking the scroll to Congress with 20,000 names of people asking for the ballot. And when she finally was received, the scroll was rejected because most of the names were women's names. If they had been men's names, it probably would have been accepted.

"Just yesterday in the Equal Rights publication I receive every month, it reproduced one of her cartoons. It's a statue of Lincoln bestowing liberty on a black man crouching below holding up his hand. And just below that, there is a member of Congress—he's got a tight mouth and he's holding up his hand with a very severe expression on his face before a woman crouching exactly as the slave before Lincoln. She is chained, and he is saying 'no.' It's a beautiful cartoon.

"I remember admiring my grandmother and my aunt very much. They both worked 35 years for the American government. My grandmother was one of the first women to be hired by the American government. In my book *Being Genuises Together*, there's a reproduction of her contract with our government. She was paid $1,200 a year. Earlier in her life, at the age of sixteen, my grandmother had been a schoolteacher in the Kansas prairies and she married very young. She married the Supervisor of Schools, who was very much older than she, and then she had two little girls, my mother and her sister, in Topeka, Kansas. I don't even know what my grandmother's name was before she was married. As a married woman she was Eva S. Evans. She apparently left her husband, the School Supervisor, which was a very unusual thing to do in those days, and went to Washington to get a job with the government, and took her two daughters with her.

"My sister and I were surrounded by these articulate women who were also very gentle and non-violent. My mother was both strong and modest, and I always felt in a way that I was her mother and that she was my child. She was amazing. I mean she never had any education and yet she knew everything by intuition.

"She never had contacts with the kind of people she admired, at least in the beginning of her life. Yet she knew that Brancusi was one of the great sculptors of our time. She knew Marcel Duchamp was a great painter. She took me to the Armory exhibit in New York in 1913. At the Armory exhibit she showed me Marcel Duchamp's *Nude Descending the Staircase*, which they had to have police protection for because people were throwing eggs and tomatoes at it—it was such a radical painting. And she knew composers, and books, and she would read to me Norman Angell, who was never terribly well-known but was one of the great English political commentators. She had all his books.

"During our childhood, when we were quite young, my paternal grandfather (referred to as Puss in my short stories), my father, and my mother would take turns reading to my sister and me in the evening. And it's very interesting, the books they would choose. I remember my mother read us all of Jane Austen and it took her quite some time, a year or more. She suggested, which was a very good idea, that we draw pictures to illustrate the books as she read them to us. And my father read us Robert Louis Stevenson's *Treasure Island*, and other books of that sort. My grandfather read us, for some reason which I've never been able to work out, all the Scandinavians.

"I myself couldn't read and I couldn't write until I was about six or seven. It was a very strange situation. I didn't start to read really a lot until I married my second husband Lawrence Vail, and I was then in my twenties. But I had been writing for a long time. I think the reason I wrote so much was I didn't realize that everyone had said it all before. It had all been said. But not having read many books, I thought I had to say it.

"I don't believe in craft. As that wonderful Japanese man who was interned in California said, if you are a serious writer you write with your heart's blood. You don't worry about craft. You don't worry about grammar and all that sort of thing. That's what irritates me in creative writing classes. I will be giving my last one in Boulder, Colorado, in about two weeks, and I always tell my students never, never, never take another creative writing course. It's most destructive, terribly destructive. What is the use of obeying the rules, following the textbooks, if your voice doesn't sound different from other people's voices?

"I want to tell you about one young man, a young professor in Eastern Washington, where I was this winter and where my beloved Grace Paley came for two days. She and I sat in on one of his classes, and everything he said to the students about craft bothered us very much. And as we were leaving, he said 'I would like very much to ask both of you to suggest a text on the novel.' He said 'I've got a textbook on poetry, one on the short story, and I need one on the novel.' And both Grace and I looked at each other and didn't know what to say. Then Grace said, 'Just ask them to write and not follow the rules, because you know the editor of the publishing house will do the worrying about punctuation.'

❧

"One of my problems with Eastern Washington University arose when they wrote to me last year and asked me to come and be a 'distinguished writer' in quotation marks. They said they had

$1,500 to give me to bring five prominent women writers on campus while I would be there. Fifteen hundred dollars! Divided among five!

"So I told them that Maya Angelou would love to come because she's a close friend, but she gets $3,000 for one lecture. Grace Paley gets $2,000. Jessica Mitford, who is another of my very dear friends, would come for $2,500. So Grace Paley, like an absolute angel, said, 'If you can get $1,500 raised to $2,000, I'll come because it would give us a couple of days together, which would be nice.' So she came for $2,000 and paid her air fare from New York out of it.

"It is true, as I said in *Being Geniuses Together*, that I am very hard on women writers. I'm hard on myself. And I'm hard on other women writers too. In *Being Geniuses Together*, I wrote that I had come to demand a great deal of women and more of women writers. It was an actual pain in the heart when they failed to be what they themselves had given their word they would seek to be. I still feel that way. I don't think we have the right, as women writers, to be unworthy or to be weak, even if we women haven't got the same long tradition as male writers. It's up to us to create it and maintain it.

"I said in *Being Geniuses Together* that I didn't admire the work of Katherine Mansfield very much, but Marianne Moore was one of my passions, and Carson McCullers too. I liked *The Heart is a Lonely Hunter* and *The Ballad of the Sad Café*, but after that I felt Carson McCullers became one of those people who are unfortunate victims of American publishers and publicity. She took reviews terribly seriously. She died much too young because she agonized so and worried so about her place in literature. And, of course, today there are several woman writers whom I admire greatly, like Grace Paley and Maya Angelou and Toni Morrison. And I liked Maxine Hong Kingston's *Woman Warrior* very much.

"I think Toni Morrison is really fantastic. And her opening speech at the Writers' Congress last year in New York was simply unbelievable. The courage of that woman, who is employed by Random House, where she has worked for years, blasting the big publishers. The whole thrust of her introduction was 'Why have we writers been so intimidated by publishers? How do publishers get this power over us?' And she said, 'We are like toys. If we act well, they're very kind to us. And if we don't do what they think we're going to do with our next book, we're cast aside.' She was, as many writers were, agitating for a writers' union, which is now a reality."

When asked about the situation for writers on the West Coast, Boyle replied, "Major writers have not yet emerged in the Bay area, like the Paris figures of the twenties, such as Joyce and Stein. I don't consider Hemingway a great writer. Not for a moment. I think maybe we will discover that there is a great writer somewhere in the Bay area who is not being published or will be published later on. Of course, we tend to over-romanticize the Paris period. It was not a particularly happy time for expatriates, and the great emphasis for going there was not, as far as I can see, any romantic notion, but the terrific dollar exchange. Our money was worth God knows how much then. You know, we could live on practically nothing. And then when the dollar was not so advantageous with the franc, people moved on to Germany, then Greece, and other places. I think Paris in the twenties was largely an economic thing.

"The belief that all the expatriates who were over there in the twenties and thirties lived in Paris is completely wrong. Most of us lived outside Paris and came in occasionally, once a month or every six weeks, to see friends or to do what business we had to do. Living in Paris was not a common thing at all among the expatriates.

"Joyce lived in Paris but saw practically no one. Hart Crane lived there and was always drunk and always in trouble and very tragic. I met Samuel Beckett in 1930, after I was married to Laurence Vail. Beckett and I met at the apartment of an American poet, Walter Lowenfels, and I have absolutely no memory of that evening except sitting in the middle of the sofa with this young man, Sam, and talking, talking, talking. We talked, I think, from nine in the evening until about one-thirty in the morning. It was really an extraordinary evening because Joyce's daughter Lucia had just been taken to the sanitarium that day or the day before. I was very close to her. We had studied dancing together with Elizabeth Duncan, Isadora Duncan's sister, and I knew that Sam had been in love with her, and so we talked about Lucia and I maintained that there is no such thing as madness. In my total ignorance, I said that it just didn't exist—that if Lucia had been loved enough and understood enough, this wouldn't have happened. Sam, very gently as he always is, still is, had worked in asylums, as you can gather from his novels, and he said—I remember the words so well—'There is an abyss and when a person goes over that abyss, love can't bring them back; emotion can't bring them back; understanding can't bring them back. It has to be something else. God knows what the solution is, but it has to be a professional approach; it can't be an emotional one.' And finally, about one-thirty in the morning, he convinced me, which I absolutely hesitated to believe before, that there is such a thing as madness. And we have since talked a lot about this conversation, because we have always had this first meeting as a kind of touchstone. Just this past Christmas he wrote, 'The thing that I will never forgive is that I wanted to talk to you about the Machiavelli play I had seen the night before and tell you the plot of it, and you wouldn't listen to me. You wanted to talk about Lucia all the time.' I don't remember about the Machiavelli at all. But he is really an extraordinary man and very like Joyce in that same gentle, modest, withdrawn sense. I found Joyce that way, and I'm amazed when I hear reports of how arrogant he was. I never knew that side of him. Another thing they had in common, Joyce and Beckett, was that they both had a very close circle of friends and kept that circle all their lives. I've been a friend of Sam's for over fifty years, and we write to each other regularly. We see each other whenever I go to Paris and it's a good relationship.

"I'm writing a long poem for him now. Unfortunately, at the present time—I think he is two or three years younger than I—he is so obsessed with death, it just terrifies me. Terrifies me. Like when he wrote me at New Year's, he said 'I can do without 1982.' Deep depression. And so this poem exhorts him not to think of death. One portion of it has appeared in a magazine called *Conjunctions*, and another section in Eastern Washington University's publication *Willow Springs*.

"Neither Beckett nor Joyce ever wanted to talk about their birthplace—Ireland. I read recently in one of Joyce's letters, 'When I die, the word Dublin will be written on my heart.' But they left Ireland. They rejected Ireland. And I have a good Anglo-Irish friend named James Stern, a very good short story writer, and I wanted him to come meet me this summer in Ireland. We're exactly the same age, born in 1902. He said, 'Something happens to me when I get on Irish soil, I can't stand it.' and that's the way it is with Beckett. That's the way it was with Joyce. But Joyce did go back to Ireland forty years later to get married. He married Nora and that was forty years after they had been living together abroad. And Beckett says he does go back for funerals.

"You know, Joyce's daughter, Lucia, died last December, still in a mental hospital. Giorgio, the son, died of cancer, but their bitterness about their father really destroyed them both when they were young. I couldn't understand it, and Giorgio used to say, 'Well, suppose you were walking up the Boulevard Montparnasse and somebody stops you and says, "Aren't you the son of James Joyce?" It's enough to drive you crazy.' And Lucia was the same way. I remember she said, 'My father's so well known—he's better known than Rabelais, and it's just a terrible burden.'

"But there probably were other factors there because they

never had a home. Nora did not like to cook or do anything like that. They always lived in *pensions,* and that does something to people. Giorgio was never able to bring himself to go to see Lucia in all those years and years and years. It's really very sad. And then his big complaint about his father was that Joyce loved Irish tenors more than anything in the world. Joyce himself was an Irish tenor. Remember, he won a contest over John McCormack. But Giorgio was a baritone, almost a bass, his voice way, way down. Beautiful. And for years Joyce sent him to singing teachers in Italy and insisted he should be a tenor."

When asked how she had managed to be so prolific in France and elsewhere with all the different moves in her life, her three husbands and six children, Boyle responded, "I always would type in bed. Because we were so often in hotels, I'd always have my typewriter with me in bed. It was easier. There wasn't a table. There wasn't a chair. We never went to any grand hotels. But I don't think I could have done it in America, because it was possible, from the point of view of money, to have people help you in Europe. Like washing dishes and cooking. In the South of France, there were always little Italian girls who were there illegally, and they were just delighted to work. We could pay them just for their food and a room to live in. At first, when my first husband, who was French, decided to return to France in 1924, we lived in the countryside near Le Havre and I did all the work myself. I mean he had a very small salary. But my husbands were always totally helpful to me, always concerned about my having time to work.

"As for my second husband, Laurence Vail, he had such terrific qualities, and when I think of the horrible stories Peggy Guggenheim (who was married to him before me) wrote about him, I wish I were younger and had longer to live so I could write a book about him to set the story straight. He had a Ph.D. from either Oxford or Cambridge, I forget which, and he knew so much about art and music and books and he shared it all with me and the children. He did drink too much on occasion, but he was a wonderful father, to his daughters, at least. He was rather jealous of his son. He felt a rivalry there.

"When he and Peggy Guggenheim divorced, she allowed him to keep a magnificent gift, an Hispano-Suiza car which his mother-in-law had made especially for him, and he sold it for 100,000 francs, which was a terrific amount in those days. So we started off on that, and eventually went to the South of France to live, then to Austria, then to the French Alps. I had given up my job in Paris as a secretary to an American fashion writer and was able to sell some stories every now and then to the *New Yorker* and Laurence and I did a number of translations together.

"We had five children living with us, including their little girl Pegeen. Peggy had custody of her, but Pegeen would come for long periods. I adored her. And my daughters were close to her, and filled with grief over her suicide. I still write to Peggy's sister in a nursing home in New Orleans. And she writes me about my books. She says of all the evil books that were ever written, the worst she has ever read was Peggy Guggenheim's autobiography.

"Laurence did have this possessive thing about his daughters. No sooner would they get married, that he would start arranging for the divorce. And he succeeded. But he and I were also divorced by then. That was during the war years, and I was back in the States. I took a train with the two children from Reno, where I got the divorce, to Salt Lake City and married Joseph Franckenstein, who was in the ski troops, stationed at Leadville, Colorado.

"That was not a hard time, economically. I was making a good deal of money then, selling serials to the *Saturday Evening Post*. It was the only time I ever made money from my writing. Before, in all those years in Austria and France, we just sort of lived hand to mouth. I had never heard of a savings account. I never even had a checking account before 1941. So all this money I began to make, I just spent. And I regret that now because I wouldn't have to work quite so hard in my declining years.

"But in the fifties, my short stories were not saleable because Joseph and I were black-listed. During all that time, he couldn't get a decent job anywhere. He had been a foreign service officer, stationed in Germany, and the tragic thing was that he had a government hearing and was completely cleared by the counselor panel in Germany; but four days later Kohn and Schine, two of McCarthy's henchmen, came over to Germany to go through the files of the people who were employed there, and they fired everyone who had had a loyalty-security hearing even though they'd been exonerated, completely exonerated. And we were told to leave at once. Joseph's immediate superior wired Washington and said he couldn't run the department without Joseph, and he said to Joseph 'Don't go, you come to work every day, do not stop working. If they send someone from Washington to replace you, he'll sit beside you, but you are not going to go.' Even in the commissary, people whom I never knew would come up to me and say, 'I'd like very much to shake your hand for what you and your husband are doing.' On the other hand, there were some people who didn't speak to us anymore. So we came back to the States and we fought it for nine years, and then, with the help of William Shirer and Edgar Murrow, Joseph was reinstated with apologies.

"How many people suffered! Arthur Miller. Pete Seeger. Langston Hughes. Lillian Hellman. And how many others! But neither Joseph nor I had ever been a member of any party whatsoever, and we didn't have many Communist friends. The charges were just something that had been completely invented."

Kay Boyle moved to the West Coast in 1963, after the death of her husband. While teaching at San Francisco State University she pursued an active involvement in the anti-war movement, which is reflected in her writing of that period.

"One novel written in California, *The Underground Woman*, was about my experiences in jail during the Viet Nam War. Of course when people hear about that, they may conclude that I was involved in a very violent demonstration of some kind. It was not. Many, many people, men and women, sat in the doorways of the induction center in Oakland, California, so that the draftees could not go in. It was just a symbolic act, because naturally they took the draftees around to the back door of the induction center and got them in through that entry where there were no places where we could sit.

"The trouble with *The Underground Woman* is that it falls apart in the middle when the woman comes out of jail. She should not have come out of jail. She should have remained there. This would have made it a more interesting book. That's where the book really fails. I switched to other themes, like that of the girl who doesn't want to go home because she is afraid of her father. *That* theme didn't have a place in *that* book because the protest against the war in Viet Nam was not a sexist issue.

"Even before I came to California, I was involved in anti-war activities. In the fifties when the bomb shelters were being built on the East Coast (we were then living in Connecticut) I would go down with Dorothy Day and refuse to take shelter in New York City. All the sirens would go off, which meant the whole population of New York had to take shelter, and as many as three or four hundred of us would not take shelter. And in the early sixties, when I was at the Radcliffe Institute For Independent Study, I was one of the 'premature' anti-Viet Nam War people. Denise Levertov, who was also at the Institute that year, and I were the only two of that large group of women to protest the war in Viet Nam. We went down and spoke on the Boston Commons. So my going to jail in

California was a continuation of my protest. That's one reason why I would not want to live in Europe again because, as a foreigner, one is not able legally to protest.

"At the present time I'm compiling a book on Irish women. I'll be going to Ireland again next year to go on with my research on contemporary Irish women. The strange thing is that Irish women are much more independent and well-equipped for life than one has been led to believe. The women whose lives I've touched—there are six or seven whom I know very well now—carry on a wonderful correspondence with me. One whom I love dearly is a woman who makes the uniforms for Catholic girls' schools—I've written a chapter about her. She's had very little education, and the first night I met her, she started talking about the sounds that are all around our planet, and how the radio is inadequate because it can't capture these sounds, like the first grunted words of paleolithic man and the terrific battles of paleolithic animals, sounds which are still there, encircling the globe.

"And there is a Dominican nun, who did her dissertation on James Joyce's *Ulysses*, and another very interesting woman working in an organization called *Aim* which works for legal change on the status of women. And another, a very radical young journalist who writes very, very well. She came twice to the United States, and my son and I heard her speak in San Francisco. First she arrived in Los Angeles where she had six engagements to speak in the Irish Republican Club, but after her first talk in the Club, they cancelled the other five talks she was to give because she pleaded with the audience not to send a penny to Ireland because she said it all went for 'the lunatic killing.' And when we heard her, she was heckled by Irish-American Republicans, but she put them all in their place.

"The most fascinating of them all is a woman called Hillary Boyle. Unfortunately we are not related. She is eighty-six now, I think, and is fantastic. She's known all over Ireland. Hillary Boyle is that wonderful type of person who finds something wrong with everything. One night she was on a television program with some bishops, talking on the subject of vasectomy. The bishops and priests were speaking against it. And she asked, 'What about the castrati in Rome?' And they were taken aback and had no answer to that. Finally, one of them came to his senses and answered 'You don't seem to understand that the only ones who were castrated by the Church for the choir were boys who had had accidents, like a horse kicking them in the balls, or something of that sort.' Can you imagine all these little boys being kicked in the balls by a horse!

"Something I wrote on the Irish situation appeared in *The*

Atlantic Monthly and was chosen as one of the best short stories of 1981, much to my amazement. I didn't think of it as a short story, but my agent had sent it in. I was very glad that it was chosen because when you get old, you like to have these little things that give you confidence again that you can still write."

Asked which of her many works she preferred, Boyle answered, "I think, from a structural point of view, that my novel *Monday Night* is the one that succeeds the best as a novel, though it's not entirely successul. The further one gets away from the first person singular for recounting one's own experiences, the better it is. That's a great gift to have, to be able, in writing, to transpose your problems onto other characters who are convincing. I don't like writing about myself. I'd rather put myself in the situation of other people and write about them. Of course, in *The Underground Woman*, Athena Gregory does represent a part of me, but that's not a good book. No, it really isn't."

ℳ

"Writing, to repeat myself, is an extremely lonely and discouraging thing. I refer all my students to Albert Camus who in his life and in his work never ceased seeking to define with clarity and modesty the writer's predicament in our particular time. Let me read you a paragraph or two from one of my talks to students. Camus believed he had not the right, either as man or writer, to sever himself from the plight of other men. He believed that the miner who was exploited, the slaves of the concentration camps, whether they were in Nazi Germany or the Soviet Union or other totalitarian states—in other words, the persecuted legions throughout the world—required the testimony of those who could speak. The writer must give voice to the silence of the silenced, Camus said. Those who could speak, and by this he meant writers above all, should not in fear or evasion or in sanctimonious judgment hold themselves apart from other men. 'That is all that is perhaps asked of each of us writers, not to separate ourselves from our time,' Camus wrote. I feel that very strongly about writing, and it's the kind of thing that I try to instill in my students. Camus demanded that the voices of all those who could speak must ring out above the clamour of a world, ring out in the doomed silence of the persecuted, and in this way make the destiny of other men less lonely than before. Camus believed that a free exchange of ideas among men of all countries would make the use of the atomic bomb an impossibility. He believed, and he wrote with constancy and a dedication on this subject, that capital punishment is worse than vengeance; it is premeditated murder. He wrote that to abolish capital punishment would constitute a public declaration that society and the state are not in themselves absolute values, and that neither society nor the state have the authority ever to do what they cannot undo. In epochs such as ours, when the collective manifestations are in danger of outdoing the manifestations of the individual spirit, the writer, the artist, the believer is deeply troubled. Self-imposed exile, such as the exile of James Baldwin, or losing oneself as a member of a group, do not seem to me to be the answer.

"Chekov once put it very well. He said that writers who are immortal have one important trait in common and that is they are going somewhere and they call out to you to go with them. Every line they write, Chekov said, is permeated by a consciousness of aim, and you feel that in addition to life as it is, it is also life as it should be. He said that all good writers possess that urgent sense of direction which can also be described as a desperate longing to give another reality to the world in which we live. And as far as the question of whether the writer can change the world...this much we know: that throughout history, so great has been the fear of the power of the writer, that books have been burned in the belief that putting the flame to the printed word also destroyed the conviction that lived in the word. We know that in the sixteenth century, Martin Luther's books were burned by Royal Edict with the stipulation that all he had written was to be 'eradicated from the memory of man.' And we know that the Nazis in obedience to official orders burned 20,000 books in 1933 alone, among them the books of Thomas Mann and Einstein. In our own country, in 1938, John Steinbeck's *Grapes of Wrath* was ordered burned, and in more recent days we are witnessing an attempt to remove Studs Terkel's book *Working* from the shelves of at least one school library. Remember that Jean-Paul Sartre once described the work of Franz Kafka as a carload of dynamite standing between East and West with each side trying to wheel it into the other camp so that it would explode there. Until 1963 Moscow declared an official ban on Kafka's writing. But because of the pressure of literary critics in Yugoslavia, Poland and Hungary, two of Kafka's stories finally did appear in a Moscow periodical in 1964. It is strange, almost beyond belief, that a formidable world power like the Soviet Union would fear the publication of fiction written by a frail, tortured young man and one who moreover had been dead for many years. But such is the power of the writer."

Asked if the woman writer has any special mission or mandate given the context of the feminist movement in the last ten years, Boyle replied negatively, "No, I don't feel that at all. I feel each individual man or woman has the same responsibility. And even when I write specifically on women, on Irish women or German women, I'm not excluding men for a moment. When I talked to my students at San Francisco State about the big peace march in Belfast in the seventies, I said that many of the women walked hand in hand with their husbands. My feminist students did not want to hear that. No, I don't like to divide it up. We all know there are awful, terrible women, and there are awful, terrible men. And though women as a group have been disadvantaged, so have men. I think women and men are both victims in our society. I think the man who works all day at a bank, that man who perhaps wanted to be a poet, he's just as much a victim as the woman. He comes home at five o'clock from a bank and is just as discouraged about life as she is about the housework. I think sharing the responsibilities, as so many of these couples are doing now, is just great. The challenge will be to arrange one's life without the children having to suffer, or the husband having to suffer, or the wife having to suffer. That is the real challenge of the feminist movement."

KAY BOYLE, 1902–

Selected Bibliography
Novels
PLAGUED BY THE NIGHTINGALE. H. Smith, 1931. 2nd ed. Illinois: Southern Illinois University Press, 1966.
YEAR BEFORE LAST. H. Smith, 1931. 2nd ed. Illinois: Southern Illinois University Press, 1969.
GENTLEMEN, I ADDRESS YOU PRIVATELY. H. Smith, 1933.
MY NEXT BRIDE. New York: Harcourt, 1934.
DEATH OF A MAN. New York: Harcourt, 1936.
MONDAY NIGHT. New York: Harcourt, 1938.
PRIMER FOR COMBAT. New York: Simon and Schuster, 1942.
AVALANCHE. New York: Simon and Schuster, 1944.
A FRENCHMAN MUST DIE. New York: Simon and Schuster, 1939. 2nd ed. 1948.
HIS HUMAN MAJESTY. Whittlesey House, 1949.
THE SEAGULL ON THE STEP. New York: Knopf, 1955.
GENERATION WITHOUT FAREWELL. New York: Knopf, 1960.
THE UNDERGROUND WOMAN. New York: Doubleday, 1974.

Memoirs

Kay Boyle (with Robert McAlmon). BEING GENIUSES TOGETHER. New York: Doubleday, 1968.

Short Stories and Short Novels

WEDDING DAY, AND OTHER STORIES. H. Smith, 1930.

THE FIRST LOVER, AND OTHER STORIES. New York: Random House, 1933.

THE WHITE HORSES OF VIENNA, AND OTHER STORIES. New York: Harcourt, 1936.

THE CRAZY HUNTER. New York: Harcourt, 1940.

THIRTY STORIES. New York: Simon and Schuster, 1946.

THE SMOKING MOUNTAIN. New York: McGraw, 1951.

THREE SHORT NOVELS. New York: Beacon, 1958.

NOTHING EVER BREAKS EXCEPT THE HEART. New York: Doubleday, 1966.

FIFTY STORIES. New York: Doubleday, 1980.

Poetry

A GLAD DAY. New York: New Directions, 1938.

AMERICAN CITIZEN. New York: Simon and Schuster, 1944.

COLLECTED POEMS. New York: Knopf, 1962.

TESTAMENT FOR MY STUDENTS. New York: Doubleday, 1970.

Non-Fiction

BREAKING THE SILENCE. New York: Institute of Human Relations Press: 1962.

THE LONG WALK AT SAN FRANCISCO STATE. New York: Grove, 1970.

Juvenile

THE YOUNGEST CAMEL. Boston: Little Brown, 1939. Revised ed., New York: Harper and Row, 1959.

PINKY, THE CAT WHO LIKED TO SLEEP. New York: Crowell-Collier, 1968.

PINKY IN PERSIA. New York: Crowell-Collier, 1968.

Translations

THE DEVIL IN THE FLESH, by Raymond Radiguet. Paris: The Black Sun Press, 1932, and The Grey Walls Press: London, 1949.

BABYLON, by René Crevel (to be published in the U.S.A. in 1984.)

Diane Johnson

FROM A CONVERSATION WITH JOHNSON
AND SUSAN GROAG BELL, HISTORIAN,
SAN FRANCISCO, APRIL 28, 1983.

Just by coincidence, Diane Johnson was interviewed by her friend, Susan Bell, on her forty-ninth birthday. "Birthdays have never made me cheerful," she said. "I find them especially gloomy these days." There was, however, little in the setting of Johnson's San Francisco apartment to project a sense of gloom. With its broad view of the city's small houses and tall buildings, Johnson's San Francisco "hideout" across the Bay from the Berkeley home she shares with her husband and children allows her the solitude necessary for writing.

"Each time I get a little house, it is because I am done out of a place to work and need another one, or the last place was becoming too comfortable. But then, once I get a new place, I love to feather it. I'm not a very good housekeeper, so I find the little places really much easier for me to control, physically and imaginatively. Our main house, in Berkeley, is huge and has twenty rooms; that's too much for me. I can't fill it up imaginatively, to say nothing of taking care of it. So I try to get away to little nests, like this one.

"This is an old building built in 1907. It has a dining room, with a fireplace, which I like. I'd rather have a dining room than some other room. The ceilings are high. My children painted the dining room red, but I'm not sure it's a success. I think it may not be the right color red—it's rather dark and not the rosy color I had hoped for.

"The original paneling was painted white, and I think if left to myself, I would paint it white again to match the other room. But the last owner of this flat laboriously stripped off all the paint, acting under some reverence for redwood. And my husband said, 'What! Paint over redwood!' Obviously, he, like the previous owner, who was also a real Californian, has a reverent feeling for redwood which I don't particularly share.

"Our house in Berkeley is also 1907, and it's rather like this except that the rooms are bigger and there are more of them. Sort of

Edwardian, or semi-Victorian, and I also like it, although I'd love to have a true Victorian, one of the really wonderful San Francisco gingerbread houses. Then we have a little house at the beach, a kind of cabin made out of half logs and very simple. There's also a flat in London which we own with a friend. It sounds like a lot of nests. The London one was built in about 1830 or 1840, with a done-over kitchen, in one of those big Georgian houses. I haven't spent any time in it yet because we just got it, but I expect to. I do spend rather more time than I should just carrying shoes and things from one place to another. I suppose finally it's a stratagem for not working.

"As you know, I have four children and three stepchildren. Miraculously, all seven children seem to have gotten along quite well. Their ages dovetail in a nice way. John's oldest child was pretty much out of the house when we married, so he didn't ever really live with us, but his other two have. His daughter comes right between my two daughters, and his son was an older brother to the whole group. It worked out very well. And they're still awfully fond of each other, I think, and see each other when we're not around, even now that they're off at school or at jobs. They're all out of the nest pretty much.

"To go back to my own childhood, it was fairly orderly. My parents were middle-aged people when they had me, the first child, so they were sensible and stable, and though they weren't precisely sedentary, we always lived in the same house, and we always went to the same summer house. My aunts and uncles always lived nearby, in their same houses.

"I think that a certain view of life, which I very much obtained from my Illinois childhood, does inform my work. In a couple of my books, I have put a middle-western protagonist, always somebody who's displaced like I am, looking at the mess of today. This person remembers an orderly society from which subsequent events have seemed to depart; the characters in my novels believe that the world is at bottom an orderly one or that is the way it was meant to be; then they find themselves in confusion and they are always longing for that earlier orderly world. Probably everyone does.

"My parents had some little influence on my becoming a writer by encouraging my interest in words, in language. Was I good at telling little stories, and did they then clap and applaud? There aren't any other writers in my family, so I didn't have any models. In fact, I really didn't know that writers were still alive. I had the impression that everyone who wrote books had written them already and disappeared from earth.

"When I went to Stephens College, I didn't want to be anything.

I had no idea or plan, which is one of the reasons my parents sent me there. I think they thought it was some kind of safe, female academy near home, but also it did have various things like theaters and art programs. They hoped that I would develop an enthusiasm for something instead of dreamy reading.

"I went to Stephens when I was seventeen and left Stephens at nineteen to get married to someone who was a medical student at UCLA. So I dropped out of college, got a job to work his way through medical school, became pregnant, began to have babies, finished college, got pregnant some more, took care of babies, started taking graduate classes, started writing novels. I don't exactly remember what must have been a tremendously energized drive or whatever it took to make me do all this, or how I got to taking writing seriously and decide to become a writer. I know that I was influenced by a friend, Alison Lurie, the novelist, who was a little older and infinitely wiser. She had been to Radcliffe and understood that there were real writers and you could be one too. She was tremendously encouraging and—she was working on her first novel—proved to me by example that novel-writing was a useful activity, and that you had every right to get a babysitter or trade off with a friend to free up some hours to do your writing. She and I did that. So I was relieved of any guilt or ambivalence that I might have had about taking time to write, even though I didn't have any particular vocation or expectations. I took my writing seriously. I think I always expected that if you wrote a novel and sent it out, it would get published. It didn't occur to me, what I know to be the case now, that people write novels and don't get them published.

"I wrote one novel, between babies, which I didn't like very much, and then I wanted to do something better. I wrote what became my first published novel, *Fair Game*, which I now don't look at with much satisfaction, but at the time it got me started. It got published right away, and I didn't have to endure what most other people have to endure. I don't know if I would have stuck through years and years of disappointment of that kind.

"Getting the Ph.D. is another story. What I can say is that I was a midwestern child from a rather bookish and cultivated home. That is, though I was not the child of intellectuals, there were books and pictures around, and I developed an interest in such things, and then at Stephens, which is by no means the acme of intellectuality, there were several professors who were encouraging to me, and my first husband's parents seemed to me also the height of worldly sophistication. Anyway, I just fell madly in love with all of these intellectual things. I suddenly felt that my slight feelings of misfittedness, that I had always combatted in my little home town, were derived from the fact that there was no one like me there, or so I thought. Away from home, I became very excited. I bought my first classical record, which was something like Tchaikovsky's *Pathetique*; then I learned about Bach—so it was a very exciting time. At UCLA, I just carried on with school and took the Ph.D. as well, even with four little babies. If you take enough courses, you get a Ph.D. You just start in and keep taking courses and God knows where it ends.

"Sometimes I have written a little about the desperation of mothers of very small children, but not much. For example, in *The Shadow Knows*—that was really written from the heart, even though it was written when I was myself past that desperate stage. Men don't want to hear about maternal desperation. They certainly don't want to hear about mothers who feel trapped or panicky. Could be *their* mothers felt that way. But women know it already, so you don't have to go into it.

"Though the woman in *The Shadow Knows* does have children, I think children are quite unconnected to my work; they are put in for verisimilitude. Similarly, in other books, the characters have children because most people have children, and also they represent part of the predicament in which I put my heroines. But I never give the children any lines. They tend to get in the way. Sometimes I send them to camp in the story. The children are there, but not emotionally for me. I am very fond of my own children, but I haven't wanted to bring them into my work—or my complaints about them either. I think you wouldn't want to tell your children of the complicated nature of your feelings for them. In fact, I can't think of any woman writer who deals with those issues. Of course, many don't have children, or didn't in the past.

"Some people, like Adrienne Rich, have very much involved their children in their conversions to lesbianism. Her book about motherhood, *Of Woman Born*, must obviously have been read by Adrienne's children. That was an unusually candid work. I can't say that I'm really familiar with Rich's work otherwise—I don't read much poetry—but I did read her book on motherhood because I was going to review it.

"The women writers I most admire are mostly dead: Jane Austen, the Brontës, the ones you would expect. Of the living, I like Alison's work and I like novels by my other friends, for instance, Alice Adams or Sheila Ballantyre. I admire Joan Didion's work tremendously. You know I did a sort of interview with Joan Didion and her husband, John Gregory Dunne. It was billed as an interview, in front of a vast audience last fall. None of us understood it as such, so when we got there, we just talked. We talked about El Salvador, where they had just been, and we just continued our lunch conversation about random topics, to the irritation of the audience, I guess. I'm not sure whether it was a great success. In any case, she's one of the most conscious craftswomen artists, and I'm sure we're interested in some of the same things—form, formal matters, the problems faced by an artist in novel writing. She's interesting to talk to, and it's interesting to read her. She's innovative and intellectual as well as a very good writer.

"The kind of crises, the particular troubles that I assign to my women characters, these are not necessarily meant to be feminist complaints, although they could legitimately be construed as such. In my mind, they may be more metaphysical or general. That sounds awfully pretentious, but I guess what I mean is that I'm not trying to write manifestos about female independence, but human lives.

"It is true, though, that almost all my novels are about independent females living in a frightening and violent world, and maybe this is just my point of view, that of a timid person viewing this undoubtedly violent world. Why I have to write about it, I don't know. I'm interested in violence in society, I guess. So there is always a very independent, timid person in the midst of the book who is actually coping with the violence. But readers often misunderstand the point I am trying to make. For example, in *The Shadow Knows*, when the heroine is raped, the violence has been interpreted as a political statement about rape. I should have made myself clearer—I might have changed the rape to some other form of violence simply to preclude this being interpreted as a narrow political statement. Rape has by now been politicized and legitimately so, but at the time of writing, I wasn't really aware of it in that way, and was using rape as a metaphor. I think that a political interpretation of the ending takes away from what I did have in mind, which was, I suppose, more metaphysical.

"There's another problem that comes from having as your central character a female person. The male narrative voice is still accorded more authority. The female narrative voice is always questioned—is she crazy? Are the things she's saying a delusion, or reality? The narrator in *The Shadow Knows* was intended as an exact and trustworthy reporter of what was happening to her. But many reviewers, while in general liking her, also questioned her about her hysteria, her paranoia, her untrustworthiness. Is she mad or sane? So I began to notice that female narrators, if they're of a sexual age, of a reproductive age, of an age to have affairs, aren't considered trustworthy. They are not the perfect narrative voice because of all the prejudice against them in our society. If you have a male narrator, he can be married and a father, and these facts will not be germane to his interpretation of events. He can tell you what happened to him on a ship, or elsewhere, and unless he's demonstrably unhinged like Dostoevsky's *Man from the Underground*, what he says will by and large be believed. But a woman is always questioned, unless she's a servant and dispassionate, or a grandmother, or a little child; then her record is believed. Someone who's been elevated to a grandmother—you know, like Old Mrs. So and So next door—people will take her word for things. A woman of venerable age. It's an interesting problem for the novelist, because if you don't want to impeach your narrator at the onset by her status, then you do well to stay away from a woman of childbearing age. Nonetheless, I write about women of childbearing age, because I like to fly in the face of these prejudices and hope that I can make them authoritative and trustworthy reporters.

"When I turned from my first novels to my biography of the first Mrs. Meredith, that grew out of my dissertation on the poetry of George Meredith. In biographies of Meredith, there would always be this little paragraph about how he was first married to Mary Ellen Peacock who ran off and left him and then, of course, died, deserted and forlorn—like the woman in a Victorian story. I always thought, I bet there is her side of it too. This was when my own marriage was breaking up, and I was particularly interested in the woman's side of things. Then also I wanted an excuse to go to England, so for that very practical reason, I devised this project, to write her side of it.

"I wrote a lot of letters and eventually I went to all the record offices and got people's wills and tried to track down who might still be around descended from either Mrs. Meredith or Meredith. I did indeed find people who had tiny little bits of things to tell me. In the case of Henry Wallace, her lover, his heirs just let me dig around under the bed. I found a little packet of letters and many tiny things that had belonged to her—a paint box, with the packet of letters tied in a faded ribbon, a lock of hair....It was very affecting and wonderfully thrilling.

"I wrote that book all pretty much at once. I had researched it in pieces, because I had to go back to England a couple of times after my first time there. I was very clumsy about research in the first place and left many stones unturned which I had to go back and turn. Ada Nisbet, the Dickens scholar, was immensely helpful. She knew so much and gave me a lot of suggestions.

"For the biography of Dashiell Hammett, which is now in press, I had the help of Hammett's daughters who were very wonderful and kind and thorough in their recollections and really anxious to get the story told, but there were many other sources, whose stories conflicted and who drove me nuts; so I think I'll stick to writing the stories of long dead people. One of the reasons I wanted to do Hammett was because I thought it would be interesting to write the biography of a man.

"My next project is going to be a spy novel set in Iran, and it has a heroine who is there by herself. There are practical reasons for having her there alone. If there is a husband around, she and you have to attend to him. You have to give him his dinner and so on. Whereas, if the woman is quite alone, she can go on thinking her thoughts, or go downtown or whatever, unimpeded. In real life, I have a husband, whose dinner I have to prepare, but I am not the heroine of a novel, so I don't mind. I don't think it's less interesting in life to have a husband; it makes things more complicated and probably more interesting. But in fiction, if you have to move the character from here to there, you just have to do more arranging if you have that extra character. It's rather the same as with children. There's a husband in *Loving Hands at Home*, but he's a kind of villain, and then there's an ex-husband in *The Shadow Knows*, who is the villain. I haven't done a nice, supportive husband around the house.

"As for the settings of my novels, I set them where I live for convenience. In one of my novels, *Burning*, I did specifically choose the West Coast—Los Angeles—as the setting. That's the only time the setting hasn't just been the result of the fact that you have to put a novel somewhere. I found Los Angeles scary, and I wanted it to be a scary novel, but I don't think anyone liked it very much. For one thing, they tended to say, 'Oh, that's California. Things like that can't happen here,' and dismissed it as a book about kooks. People did like it in England. *Burning* is the one that's most California, but the others, although they are set in the West, could have been set anyplace. *The Shadow Knows*, for example, which I wrote living in England, was first set in Los Angeles, but then I decided after the reception of *Burning*, that Los Angeles was too loaded a place in the minds of readers, so I changed it to Sacramento. Nobody has ever complained about the Sacramentoness.

"People often ask me how I choose the topics of my novels, and I've never been able to answer that. They want to know how they themselves can get an idea and start out; one can point them to some sources such as where Henry James says, 'Well, I was walking by a door and I looked in and . . . .' But I don't know that there is any precise or coherent account by any writer of the whole origin of subjects, and I'm certainly not able to come up with an explanation for my choice of subjects. I know I put bits of my life in and I try to create a mood or focus on some overall subject. When I say I'm going to write a spy novel set in Iran, I'm thinking in my mind: the spy is kind of a faithless functionary, with a secret life. It's also a fruitful metaphor for modern man and also for national paranoia. Also, it is an interesting and amusing genre, which should have an exciting plot. I can articulate some of these reasons, but not all. Why set it in Iran? That's because it is an interesting place, and I was there, and also, I want to write about Americans and you can really see them better in the context of another society, the way stories of colonials depict the English.

"When I went to Iran, which was a little before the revolution, I thought, 'Gee, I'd like to write a novel about this place.' I think you save up ideas or notions that are attractive and at some right moment, you use them. This computer store of notions is what every writer has, and so you reach into your store under the impress of some other emotion or need to write. I'm wondering if I should read John Le Carre's *The Little Drummer Girl*. Writers do learn from other writers.

"I seem to have learned most from the earliest things I read, from my basic childhood school reading, from a time when I was really moved by and caught up in books, which is no longer true for me. I read them now in an entirely different way, much more critically and technically. I suppose I was most influenced by nineteenth century writers, because those are the only ones I remember we had in our local Carnegie Library. Writers like Kafka and Joyce, I did read early, but mostly I read nineteenth century writers like Alexandre Dumas. Anyway, I didn't read much modern literature. I think at a certain point, when you begin to write yourself, you're already formed and influenced. Not that you still can't be taught. Now to be taught, I go back to Kafka, Graham Greene, several English writers, who I think are extremely skillful, and the classics.

"Kafka was very important to me—is very important to me— the sense of being totally surrounded by strange forces you can't control. I try not to read too many modern novels, especially while I'm writing them, because I do find that if they're really good, that just depresses me. 'Oh no, I can never write like this!' And if they're really bad, I wonder why am I writing another novel to contribute to this sea or morass of terrible novels that have come over the transom this week. I think writers go back to the works that are safe for them, that they know to be endlessly stimulating, and yet don't really threaten them. Anyone could read Jane Austen over and over again. You know you can't be Jane Austen, and it doesn't matter somehow. People have found my writing rather gothic, but strangely enough, gothic novels of the nineteenth century didn't have any influence on my writing. What I liked were sea-going tales.

"Today, I always think it's helpful to talk about writing with other writers, for instance Alice Adams, although we write very differently. She writes short stories, which I don't do at all. I find the things that she says about the short story are helpful and interest-ing, but it doesn't help me to write short stories. I've tried a couple and can't do it. I think I am just too garrulous; I want to have the space for a slow effect. If I knew how the short story really worked, I guess I would be better able to understand why I can't or don't want to write one. I prefer to read novels too. You don't want it to be over just like that. If I'm going to write a novel and spend a couple of years at it, I get to know the people, imagine the rooms; I would feel bereft to give up my characters so soon. Usually, by the time I'm finished, I'm sick of them. I think that may be a necessary condition for finishing a novel. But when I'm reading a really good book, I don't want it to end, and I start reading more slowly.

"When you're writing, it's exciting to be finishing up. You want to see how it's going to come out, and you want to sense its shape after you're all done and you want to know if the ending is right and all of these imponderables that you can't know until you've done the ending; so you race along trying to get there.

"Like many writers, I am already imaginatively into the next project, which is really the way you protect against post-partum depression—you get pregnant again. With Virginia Woolf, who really was neurasthenic—a kind of basket case when she finished a novel—she really did have to rest and repair her energies. Us lesser sensibilities are probably sturdier peasant stock.

"Sometimes you see people who cannot finish their novels. They never get them out of the house and published. But when I sent out my first novel and it came back with this little letter saying that we can't publish it but it's nice and maybe an agent could do something with it, I was very undone. I went through a red light and got arrested, driving to school. And I think that was almost the only rejection slip I have ever gotten; I've protected myself.

"When Harcourt-Brace decided to publish *Fair Game*, I was tremendously elated. I got myself taken out to dinner. Much joy and happiness and a great feeling that my life would change and be tremendously different. Everything would be all right. It was very exciting.

"After I had published it, I found life tremendously depressing. I guess I'm like other people in that I had built such a fantasy life on what would happen when I became a real published writer. Of course, nothing happens. When I realized that nothing was going to happen, I became depressed and had my hair bleached. For about a week, I went around with this snow-white terrible peroxide hair. Then I realized that that wasn't the solution either. So I had it dyed back. I'm not so sure I was right. I probably should have stuck with blonde hair a little longer. So publication did make me feel very gloomy, but at the same time you realize the important thing is the work itself, not any kind of secondary benefit that's going to accrue. In fact, in time secondary benefits do accrue. But they don't immediately, and of course, nobody reviewed the novel. The couple of times I was invited to a bookshop to autograph it were humiliating and terrible. So publishing a novel is a very cautionary and revealing experience.

"The three or four books of mine that did the best—the ones that have been published by Knopf—have all done well in various ways, but curiously enough, *The Shadow Knows*, and *Lesser Lives* were badly reviewed and *Burning*, before that, as well.

"*The Shadow Knows* was attacked in the *Times* by a person called Karyl Roosevelt who said something like 'this woman has more trouble than you can believe. She's divorced; she has four children, and not only that, she has to walk through the snow storm, carrying them, etc.'—all the things that women do in fact have to do. I was very interested in the fact that the things she most objected to were in fact the most literal depictions of what I take to be very common aspects of female life. And it was a woman who was reviewing it! But that book was then well reviewed in the *Daily Times* by Anatole Broyard and his review, which has been quoted on every jacket reprint since, says something strange; he said, 'It's enough to make you want to throw yourself down at the feet of the next woman you see.' I felt that he was liking and appreciating the heroine not for the reasons I had intended, but because she was so cuddly, brave and cheerful. Maybe that is an okay appreciation— the heroine was praised and, by extension I was being praised, for the qualities of her character. It is a very common thing in male reviewers of women's books to respond to what they take to be the character of the woman author. It was Alice Adams who noticed that when people objected to her books (usually it's male reviewers), they'll object because the heroines are divorced or fat or middle class or rich or something else they disapprove of. Then they will proceed to write in a way that shows that they are talking about Alice herself and not her characters. They go on to reveal a whole set of attitudes about female behavior, and if the characters don't measure up, then the male reviewer objects on these moral and extra-literary grounds. Women, they say, should not be, or behave, like this.

"The writer wants to be praised for the management of formal and technical aspects of the narrative and wide-ranging perceptions about society and perhaps the quality of her sensibility, not her own character, and, mainly you want your book to be a success on its own terms. You don't want your personal characteristics dragged into it. If your heroine was quite an unlikeable character but came off as true, you would be just as pleased as if people said she was adorable. Of course, the heroine in *The Shadow Knows* is a likeable character, people say. I wanted her to be a likeable character. I don't think you can really write a novel with a protagonist who is truly unlikeable.

"Writing a biography is a different matter. I did not love Dashiel Hammett. In fact I had to get over a kind of aversion to him. I did come to a kind of sympathy for him, a feeling I would not, however, describe as love. There again, I had to interest myself in certain practical and technical matters of biography writing—to keep my own interest up.

"When you begin to write a biography, you should believe before you set out that you love your subject. However, be prepared for the scales to fall away later, as they surely will. You just have to get through certain parts of the character's life like a little soldier. I wondered how I was going to do Hammett's military service, for example. I expected to be bored but in fact, I found it was perfectly interesting; he wrote very amusing letters from Alaska. Undoubtedly, you stretch out the parts of a biography that interest you more and shorten the parts that don't. There's no way around that, but you do have to get through the boring parts. Novels are like that too. I, for instance, hate to do descriptions. I hate to have to bother with what the color of her dress is or even her hair, so I have to make myself describe the room, the dress, the hair. I leave it out as much as possible, but these details need to be there to a certain extent.

"I think that writing is a fairly mysterious profession. When I write, there is a kind of unconscious trance I fall into. You surprise yourself all the time. Other writers say this too. All writers I know are interested in testimonials by other writers about how they do it, how it came to them in a dream. The process is very interesting and mysterious. And I gather it's rather an attractive profession, one which lots of people think they may take up but which in fact few people do. It's a difficult profession, or vocation, but it feels natural to me.

"Some of my essays and reviews recently appeared as a book, *Terrorists and Novelists*. They are reprinted pieces that were in the *New York Review of Books* and the *New York Times* or the *T.L.S.* It's been received very kindly. I was surprised because I thought there would be some criticism, people saying who needs collected book reviews. But, in fact, there seems to be an audience for essays, if I can dignify them by that term. There are some very wonderful essayists writing now, for example, Gore Vidal and Joan Didion. I like Tom Wolfe, although many people don't. Hunter Thompson, Edward Hoaglund.

"I can tell you an amusing story about Gore Vidal and me, driving and getting lost in the hills of Hillsborough and appearing at a house where people were sitting in the dark because the lights had gone out all over Hillsborough in the wake of a power failure. People were sitting at their dining tables by candlelight, flashlight, and we shadowy figures came up to the door to ask for a phone book to look up the proper address where we were going. We were only a few doors away as it turned out, but the people were very, very suspicious of us, and Gore was rather over-cautious of them, so that it was I who had to go to the door. He didn't want to have to sign autographs. Here we were in this pitch dark, and these people by candlelight, and I didn't think they would raise too much of a clamor over him, but he lurked behind me, and never did reveal himself to them. The people would have been delighted if they had known who he was. It would have made an entirely wonderful story for them to tell later. Now I forget the point of this anecdote. It had to do with my admiration for Gore's essays.

"I have been asked how I deal with my writing and my teaching, whether they interact or conflict with one another. They conflict, and what I've done over the years is withdraw from teaching little by little, so now I don't teach very much, and I find that I can get more writing done. My situation at U.C. Davis now is a half-time job in which I teach in two years what I otherwise would have taught in one. In practical terms, this gives me several quarters completely off and summers as well, and I think it's going to work out better. Before that, I just tried to get grants and cadge years off as best I could.

"Sometimes I like to teach when I'm not writing, because I do find it stimulating and it makes me work up things or get into new things, but mostly I'd rather not do it. Reviewing books provides some of the same intellectual challenges. Anyway, reviewing makes you go to the library and get things read, and it suits my more lazy nature; also I'm rather frightened of classes, especially large ones. I quite like my graduate creative writing class because we can sit around and talk about writing, but a huge lecture about Brontë puts me into fits.

"I've found that students rarely ask questions about my work. They're very much more interested in their own work. Maybe this is the natural egotism of writers. If they've read my work, they tend to be people who are reverent to writers and who want to be one themselves, so they try to find out what a writer's like and do all the apprentice work. But very many writing students don't even bother to read. I think they're so used to creative writing classes—they've been through a mill of them—that they just think of the teacher as a kind of functionary and not as an independent person with a life or career. This may be California; it may be different at Yale or elsewhere.

"I dislike the term 'creative writing,' although I can't think of another term. I don't really think one can teach it. You can teach technical things necessary to good writers, but you can't make writers out of people who aren't writers. I think that probably in America, which is so large, unlike England, which is so small, writers have to work hard to find each other, need little places of assembly. So the main point of 'creative writing' classes is to provide a kind of collegial setting where people can meet. Now the Bay area is really quite a center for writers. There is a great deal of writing going on here. And most of the writers know each other, hang around with each other to a certain extent in different little coteries.

"As for some of the big name feminist writers, I don't know them very well. Kate Millett is very sympathetic and nice and Germaine Greer a bit scary and formidable. I read Kate Millett's first book, *Sexual Politics*, and a bit of her next one, the come out of the closet one. Then I couldn't read the one about the girl who was murdered in the basement; that was too much. I looked at Germaine Greer's book about women painters because that interests me, but I'm not a great reader of political feminist works. It's like preaching to the converted and you only have so much time to read.

"Sometimes I think that the term feminist has become counter productive and that one has to be a bit more subtle in working for women if anything is to get done. I don't deny being a feminist, but I believe the term has become compromised in some way. All isms are easy targets for their opposition. Communism, environmentalism, you know. 'Ism' characterizes a kind of idealogue and all the attendant inflexibility. Maybe people just don't want to be characterized. Still I believe that every fully conscious woman is at heart a feminist, whether she calls herself that or not. Lots of women (I'm finding out now)—lots of young women in their twenties deny being feminists; they just take for granted the gains which feminism has provided for them, but it may just be the term itself or that the particular set of attitudes that it conveyed to us no longer conveys the same things to young women today."

DIANE JOHNSON, 1934–

Fiction

FAIR GAME, Harcourt, Brace & World, New York, 1965.

LOVING HANDS AT HOME, Harcourt, Brace & World, New York, 1968; Wm. Heinemann, Ltd., London, 1969; Ballantine Books (paperbound edition), New York, 1972.

BURNING, Harcourt Brace Jovanovich, Inc., New York, 1971; Wm. Heinemann, Ltd., London, 1971.

"An Apple, An Orange" [short story], EPOCH, Vol. XXX, No. 1(Autumn 1971), 26–40.

THE SHADOW KNOWS, Alfred A. Knopf, New York, 1974; The Bodley Head, London, 1974. Sections reprinted in forthcoming anthology WOMEN WRITING (W.J. Morrow, n.d.). THE SHADOW KNOWS, Pocketbooks, New York, 1980; Granada, London, 1980.

LYING LOW, Alfred A. Knopf, Inc., Autumn 1978.

Non-Fiction

"Lady in the Shadow of Great Lives," SAN FRANCISCO CHRONICLE—THIS WORLD, December 3, 1972.

"The Case for Patty Hearst," THE NEW YORK REVIEW OF BOOKS, XXIII:7(April 29, 1976), 15–17.

Preface to facsimile edition of John Ruskin's "King of the Golden River"; Charles Dickens, "A Holiday Romance"; and Tom Hood, "Petsetilla's Posy"; Garland Publishing, Inc., New York and London, 1976.

Preface to facsimile edition of Margaret Gatty, PARABLES OF NATURE, Garland Publishing, Inc., New York and London, 1976.

Preface to George Sand, MAUPRAT, da Capo Press, New York, 1977.

Interview with Gore Vidal, NEW YORK TIMES BOOK REVIEW, April 17, 1977, pp. 1, 47.

TERRORISTS AND NOVELISTS [collected essays], Alfred A. Knopf, New York, 1982.

Numerous reviews in SAN FRANCISCO CHRONICLE, NEW YORK REVIEW OF BOOKS, WASHINGTON POST, CHICAGO TRIBUNE, and elsewhere.

Biography

LESSER LIVES: THE TRUE HISTORY OF THE FIRST MRS. MEREDITH, Alfred A. Knopf, New York, 1973; Wm. Heinemann, Ltd., London, 1973.

DASHIELL HAMMETT: A LIFE, (in press), Random House, (September, 1983).

Screenplays

"The Shining," adaptation of novel by Stephen King of the same name. In collaboration with Stanley Kubrick; produced by Warner Brothers.

"Grand Hotel," (completed).

ABOUT THE CONTRIBUTORS

I. WRITERS

KAY BOYLE is the author of some thirty books of fiction and non-fiction, including *Being Geniuses Together*, which describes her life in Paris in the thirties and *The Underground Woman*, which derived from her experiences in San Francisco in the sixties.

JUDY GRAHN is a poet living in California. Her poetry is collected in *The Work of a Common Woman* and *The Queen of Wands*, and is recorded on an album, "Where Would I Be Without You." She has lived in California since the sixties.

SUSAN GRIFFIN is a writer of fiction, poetry and plays. Her works include *Woman and Nature: The Roaring Inside Her*, *Pornography and Silence: Culture's Revolt Against Nature*, *Made From This Earth: An Anthology of Writings*, and the award-winning play, *Voices*. She is a native Californian living in Berkeley.

DIANE JOHNSON is a novelist, biographer, critic and Professor of Literature at the University of California at Davis. She was born in Illinois and has spent most of her adult life in California. Her best known works are her novels, *The Shadow Knows* and *Lying Low*, and her biography of Mary Ellen Peacock: *Lesser Lives*. She is a frequent contributor to the *New York Times* and the *New York Review of Books*, and essays from these periodicals are collected in *Terrorists and Novelists*.

MAXINE HONG KINGSTON has written *The Woman Warrior* and *China Men*. She grew up in Stockton, California and currently makes her home in Hawaii.

URSULA LEGUIN is an internationally-acclaimed writer of science fiction. Some of her most popular books are *The Left Hand of Darkness*, *The Lathe of Heaven*, *The Dispossessed*, *The Orsinian Tales*, and *The Earth Sea Trilogy*. She grew up in Berkeley and currently resides in Portland, Oregon.

JANET LEWIS is a novelist and poet, author of *The Invasion, The Wife of Martin Guerre, Against a Darkening Sky, The Trial of Soren Quist, The Ghost of Monsieur Scarron* and *Poems New and Old* (1918--1980). She has been a member of the Stanford community for more than half a century.

138

TILLIE OLSEN is the author of *Tell Me a Riddle, Silences,* and *Yonnondio.* Born in Nebraska, she has lived in the Bay area since the thirties.

JOYCE CAROL THOMAS is a poet, playwright and novelist, the author of *Inside the Rainbow* (poetry) and *Marked by Fire* (novel), for which she received a National Book Award in 1983. She was born in Oklahoma and has spent her adult life in Northern California.

JESSAMYN WEST is best known as the author of *The Friendly Persuasion, Massacre at Fall Creek, The Woman Said Yes* and *Double Discovery.* Born in Indiana, she was raised in Southern California and has lived most of her adult years in the Napa Valley.

II. INTERVIEWERS

SUSAN GROAG BELL is an historian, an Affiliated Scholar at the Center for Research on Women at Stanford University and a visiting lecturer in the Department of History. Her published books include *Women from the Greeks to the French Revolution* and Women, the Family and Freedom: The Debate in Documents, 1750–1950.

BRIGITTE CARNOCHAN is a graduate student in English at the University of California, Berkeley, and a sometime lecturer at Stanford University. She is currently writing a biography of Janet Lewis.

JENNIFER CHAPMAN graduated from Stanford in 1981 and has since taught English in Indonesia and The People's Republic of China. She was a student intern at the Center for Research on Women (CROW) on the West Coast Women Writers project.

MARGO DAVIS is a photographer and Assistant Director of the Stanford Instructional Television Network. Her photographs have appeared in numerous exhibitions and are represented in several major collections. Her book *Antigua Black; Portrait of an Island People* appeared in 1973.

JOHN FELSTINER is Professor of English at Stanford University. His publications include works on Latin American poetry, the literature of the holocaust, and books titled *The Lies of Art: Max Beerbohm's Parody and Caricature* and *Translating Neruda: The Way to Macchu Picchu.*

ARTURO ISLAS is Associate Professor of English at Stanford University. He has edited *Miquzitl,* a collection of Chicano student fiction, and has written two as yet unpublished novels, *Day of the Dead/Dia de los Muertos* and *Reason's Mirror.*

NANNERL KEOHANE is the President of Wellesley College. At the time of the CROW dialogues, she was Associate Professor of Political Science at Stanford University. Her publications include articles on French philosophers and a book titled *Philosophy and the State in France: The Renaissance to the Enlightenment*.

ANN MELLOR is Professor of English at Stanford University. She is the author of numerous articles on English romantic literature and two books titled *Blake's Human Form Divine* and *English Romantic Irony*.

DIANE MIDDLEBROOK is Professor of English at Stanford University. She is author of *Walt Whitman and Wallace Stevens, Worlds into Words: Understanding Modern Poems* and numerous poems.

MARILYN YALOM is Deputy Director of the Center for Research on Women at Stanford University and a lecturer in Modern Thought and Literature. She was for many years Professor of Foreign Languages and Literature at the California State University at Hayward. She has written on a number of French and American nineteenth and twentieth century writers and has jointly edited two other CROW-sponsored books, *Victorian Women* and *Rethinking the Family*.

PHOTOGRAPHER'S NOTE

Through the years, many friends have asked me to comment about how I make a photographic portrait. The easy answer is, of course, the technical one...with a Hasselblad and a fine-grain film, with a marvelous north light if I'm lucky and an unrushed moment.

The more complex response requires another level of discussion. What is it that moves me to click the shutter at a decisive moment or to select a certain image when editing a proof sheet? I think it is the recognition of a connection between the photographer and the person being photographed. In this process, the elements of artistic integrity and emotional dynamism join with a likeness and merge in one image, making all others seem trivial. It becomes very difficult for me to relate to the other images once this evolution has taken place. This one photograph, the portrait, takes on a life of its own. It is an interpretation by the photographer, it becomes a document for history, it reflects a biography at a certain point in time.

It is no longer clear to me that the degree of familiarity with the subjects determines the strength of the portrait. I used to believe, like the French photographer, Nadar, that the person I know best is the one I photograph best. I have since come to question this belief. I have had the privilege of knowing as friends only three of the ten women authors in this book: Kay Boyle, Joyce Carol Thomas and Janet Lewis. I had but a couple of hours to photograph the other authors. In some cases, I was able to read their books, in other cases there was no time. However, in those brief meetings, I felt a common understanding: that even though we knew very little about each other as individuals, we knew about each other as artists. And that even though we come from different disciplines, whether it be words or photographs, we are involved in a similar process of expression and interpretation.

—MARGO DAVIS